Oracle DBA 101:

A Beginner's Guide

Rao R. Uppaluri

Oracle DBA 101: A Beginner's Guide

ISBN: 1-58112-764-2

Universal Publishers/uPUBLISH.com
2000

www.uPUBLISH.com/books/uppaluri.htm

Preface

After simmering in the dynamic waters of research in Chemistry and Physics for nearly four decades, I first entered the field of business software as a hobby. This hobby turned into passion and took me to several areas such as Oracle 7.x, Oracle DBA, Developer 2000, Visual Basic 4.0 and Visual basic 5.0. I found that most of the books were written by stalwarts who were mathematically oriented and hence treated the topics in a dry fashion. Hence I had to read each topic myriad times to make sense. The present monograph on Oracle DBA is a treat of the topic in "English", with examples from day-to-day experience and is ideal for newcomers to this field. This may be an oversimplified approach. In the process of simplification, rigour is the first casuality. However, I realise how difficult it is to discover examples that truly resemble any real-life situation. I have tried to give such examples that enable the reader to grasp the concepts.

This book is organised as follows. Chapter 1 discusses Oracle database in general and different components that go to make an *Instance*. Chapter 2 describes the estimation of the size of *Non-clustered* and *Clustered Tables*. Chapters 3 describes routine monitoring including *Tablespace Allocations, Freespace, Fragmentation* along with some related *Views*. In Chapter 4, preventive measures to avoid problems in the database are discussed. Chapter 5 includes a very important aspect of Oracle, viz., *Security*. In view of its paramount importance, a more detailed discussion is given exclusively for *Rollback Segments* in Chapter 6. Several aspects of *Backup* and *Recovery* and comparison of different *Backup* processes are presented in Chapter 7. Chapter 8 gives a flavour of *Audit* in Oracle. The concluding chapter provides examples of minor changes in the code of application programs that result in optimal utilisation of resources.

As newer versions of Oracle become available, the need to write scripts for Database Tuning etc will not be necessary since they will come in packages. However, what these packages do inside the "box" will become clear after going through this book. Hence this book will be an useful tool at the introductory level for the Teacher as well as the Taught in Oracle classes.

I scrupulously avoided the usage of words like "Table" and phrases such as "For instance" in the conventional sense since these have different connotations in Oracle. Instead, I used "Illustration" and "For example". All English terms not used in the conventional sense as well as Oracle keywords are italicised.

I believe that after going through this elementary monograph, reading other books by software giants like Kevin Loney, J B Greene and M R Ault may not be that initimidating. These authors have greatly influenced my thinking on this topic.

I would like to thank several people who made the writing of this book possible. Renuka Uppaluri my daughter, always had tremendous confidence in my capabilities, which I some times felt, was probably not justified. Even today, she feels the same. Without her encouragement, I would never have even entered the field of software. My other daughter, Prasanti Uppaluri feels equally about my capabilities but strongly feels that at this age, I deserve to rest rather than maintain this arduous schedule; but she never comes in my way. My wife, Vardhani Uppaluri like any house-maker, is neutral. Neither she has confidence in me nor is disappointed by me. But I can not imagine my life without all three.

Seelam Venkat Reddy one of my associates during Oracle/Developer course was my constant companion in developing an application program on Integrated Bank Branch Management. He was an exceptional student, not in a hurry to cross the seas until he had learnt enough. During this development, we learnt many tricks in Oracle, the hard way. It was a great experience. This gave a fillup for future endeavours including this monograph.

I have had the pleasure of learning the Oracle/Developer Course from M/S Syspro (XL Computers Ltd), Bombay, India, under the management of Mukul Gupta. He was kind enough to allow unlimited access for practicals as part of the course. I benefited tremendously from this facility. In addition, he also provided a facility for Oracle DBA practicals for a small fee. This helped a lot in understanding the topic.

4

Two practicing Oracle DBAs, Srinivas Sunkara, NC, USA and Ajit Nadgir, NJ, USA, kindly read the manuscript and provided a few comments. Renuka Uppaluri has painstakingly proof-read the manuscript for spelling and grammatical mistakes. Havish Koorapaty, my son-in-law, helped with the formatting of this book and I am thankful for his patience in performing this task that required several iterations.

Most of the material and ideas in this booklet originated from the Oracle Corporation's materials and books by the authors Ault, Greene and Loney. I added my simplified interpretation to these. I am indebted to the Corporation and these authors for the same. Oracle is a registered trademark of Oracle Corporation.

I am responsible for all omissions and commissions in the interpretation of the topic and in the manuscript.

I shall be grateful to any reader who can provide critical comments and suggestions which will go in improving this book in serving the purpose for which it was written, viz., simplification of the topic. My email address is ruppaluri@hotmail.com. Finally, I would like to thank Universal Publishers/uPUBLISH.com for accepting this book for publication.

Rao R Uppaluri
May-October 1999
Milwaukee,WI and Cary, NC, USA

Table of Contents

List of Illustrations

Chapter 1   Oracle Database

An Oracle database is a set of data. This set is stored and is accessed in a manner consistent with Relational Model. By database, one refers to a physical database along with physical objects, memory objects, and process objects. Data in a database is stored in *Tables*. Relational *Tables* are defined by their columns. An Oracle database stores its data in *Files*. Internally they are database structures that provide a logical mapping of data to files, allowing different data to be stored separately. These logical divisions are called *Tablespaces*. A database can have several *Tablespaces* as depicted in Illustration 1.1.

Illustration 1.1 - My Database's Tablespaces

In a typical database I dealt with, the *Tablespaces* are named as *Org_Name* (Name of organisation), *System, User_Data, Temporary_Data, RBS_Data* etc. Each *Tablespace* has a specific purpose. For example, *System Tablespace* contains what is called a *Data_Dictionary*, a sort of an information centre about the data, data type, length, precession and database objects (e.g., *Tables, Indexes, Synonyms, Views, Grants, Roles* etc.). Thus, *Data_Dictionary* gives almost complete information about all aspects of the database content. *Data_Dictionary* is an important source of information about the database and hence its contents should not be accessible to all. It is like an inventory list of items in a jeweller's shop.

A *Tablespace* is a logical division of a database. A given database must have at least one *Tablespace* to start with. This essential *Tablespace* is known as *System Tablespace* (like a Government Office) from where the database is run. A *Tablespace* can belong to one and only one database. In Illustration 1.1, *User_Data* is a *Tablespace* which is used to contain several *User's* data. *RBS_Data* is yet another *Tablespace*.

Each *Tablespace* contains one or more *Files* called *Datafiles* (e.g., *Table*). A given *Datafile* (also called *Segment*) can belong to one and only one *Tablespace*. *Datafiles* are fixed in size at the time of creation. As the data grows in the file, and more space is needed, new files are added. The different possible segments are: *Table Segment*, *Index Segment*, *Rollback Segment* and *Temporary Segment*.

Dividing database objects among multiple *Tablespaces* allows these objects to be physically stored in separate *Datafiles*, which are placed on separate disks. For example, *Data_Dictionary Table*s which provide a catalogue, are used by the *System* to manage itself. All *Data_Dictionary Tables* are stored in the *System Tablespace* and are accessed by one *User*, *Sys* (equivalent to a Government Official). *User Sys* owns the *Data_Dictionary Tables*. The *User System* owns the *Views* that access these *Data_Dictionary Table*s for use by the rest of the *Users* in the database. It may be recapitulated that a *View* is a *Selection* of one or more rows from one or more *Tables*. The data is not duplicated. This means that the *View* does not occupy any storage space in the database. The *View* can neither be altered nor can any *Indexes* be *created* on any columns of the *View*. The definition of *View* (including the query that *created* it, its column lay out, and the *Privileges granted* on it) is stored in the *Data_Dictionary* of the database.

In my database, *Datafiles* of all *Users* are stored in different folders in the *Tablespace, User_Data*. Any database internally comprises *Schema, Tables, Users, Indexes, Clusters, Hash-clusters, Views, Sequences, Procedures, Packages, Triggers, Synonyms, Privileges, Roles, DB Links, RBS* etc. Since these are relatively simple and known to all the Oracle *Users*, they are not dealt with here. *Privileges and Roles* are discussed later (Sections 5.2 and 5.5).

In addition to the above items, the database also contains internally two memory structures known as global area and process area. The global area comprises *SGA* which consists of *Db_Block* buffer, *Dictionary_Cache*, *Redolog* buffers, *Shared_SQL_Pool*. The process area comprises the database's own background processes, managed by the database itself. These process structures are *SMON, PMON, LGWR, CKPT, ARCH* etc. These require a little exposition.

1.1 Memory Structures

As was mentioned before, there are two kinds of memory structures available in Oracle. They are global area and process area. The most important of these is the *System Global Area* (SGA). This is a composite of different sub memory areas within as indicated in Illustration 1.2.

Db_Block buffer	Redolog buffer	Dictionary_ Cache	Shared_SQL_ Pool

Illustration 1.2 - Structure of SGA in Oracle 7

The *SGA* is like a bulletin board. Its use can be understood as follows. The most efficient way of communicating information to all employees in an organisation is to exhibit the information on the notice board. As and when new information is to be communicated, old information is removed to make space for the new information. The memory areas are like the bulletin board. Let us see what each of these sub memory areas is for.

Db_Block buffer, as the name suggests, is a temporary (buffer) memory location in the *SGA* to hold the data blocks read by the server process from the segments (such as *Tables, Indexes*) of the database through an SQL query. This buffer occupies roughly 30%

of the *SGA* size. The size of this buffer is fixed and can be changed at will, if need arises. Since in a query such as:

```
SQL> Select * from Tn where parameter1 = m;
```

only a part of the *Segment* (*Table Tn*) of the database is read, the size of this buffer is smaller than the size of a database segment. So this buffer can not continue to keep all the data brought into it by all the queries. Like the bulletin board above, all old information is to be selectively wiped out to make room for the recent information. The buffer uses what is called Least Recently Used (**LRU**) algorithm to wipe out old information to make space for the new information.

We all use this LRU algorithm in every day life unknowingly. Suppose there is space for only two photo albums in the coffee table of your living room. When you are just married, you keep the engagement album and the wedding album. These are the most currently referred to albums by your visitors. After a few years, a child is born and a new album of the child gets filled and it takes the prime place on the coffee table. Due to lack of space, the engagement album goes to the storage, since it is the least recently referred to, i.e., LRU. With time, another child is born and the wedding album goes to storage and the second child's album takes its place. And so on so forth. At some later date, may be on your 25th wedding anniversary, you may look at your old wedding album and you get it from the storage. It stays in the living room till some other album takes its place. Whichever is the least recently referred to, will go to storage. This is exactly what happens in the *Db_Block* buffer. The data that is most recently used goes to the top while the least recently used goes to the bottom of the queue. If new data comes in, it enters on the top and the bottom most one, that is least recently used, is sent to the disk.

One may wonder why the bulletin board is required at all. All the information to be disseminated may be kept in a central (database) place for all employees to go and refer. The central place has all old as well as new bulletins (database). This will result in tremendous wastage of time if every employee has to go to the office, rummage through all the notices and get the most recent one. Instead it is lot faster if a copy of the only the most recent and important one is kept handy near a central place, i.e., the bulletin board. Similarly memory space access is much faster than disk access for a database. This is made use of in a sequence. In Oracle, one may recall that a *Sequence* is *created* by the following:

```
SQL> Create sequence abc
     minvalue 1 maxvalue 5000
     cache 10;
```

The *Sequence* is *created* in the database on the disk. Everytime you wish to draw a number from the *Sequence "abc"* you have to visit the database. Instead, while creating the *Sequence*, a Cache parameter 10 was chosen. That means a set of ten next following numbers are brought over from the database and kept handy in the memory space. Then the next ten numbers at any time are drawn from the memory space and this avoids as many trips (I/O traffic reduction) to the database. The memory space visits are much faster than the database visits.

1.2   Shared SQL Pool

In the Oracle 7 version, the above referred to *Data_Dictionary_Cache* is inside the *Shared_SQL_Pool*, which constitutes about 10-20% of the *SGA* size. In this pool, SQL statements run against the database are stored, in addition to their execution plan. When an identical SQL query is posed, this pool makes the execution of the query faster by providing the execution plan as well as the parse tree for the query.

1.3   Dictionary Cache

Data_Dictionary_Cache, as mentioned earlier, is an information link to the database. It has access to complete information about all database objects. If a *Table* is queried by a *User*, this cache is first referred to before the query is answered. The cache checks with the *Data_Dictionary Tables* in the database, if the database object of the query exists. If so, it checks where, and whether the *User* is authorised to query the object and whether the information asked for is in the object. Such information about that object is temporarily stored in the cache and such information grows. This information in the cache is also managed via LRU algorithm (explained above). Thus information about frequently referred to database objects exists in this cache for next *User* without repeating the visit to the database. This is how the process becomes faster. If the *Data_Dictionary_ Cache* is set too small (i.e., the *Data_Dictionary Table* information brought into it is very small), the *Data_Dictionary Tables* have to be queried often in the database. These queries are called **recursive hits**. Thus the *Data_Dictionary_Cache* is an important sentinel of the database for security. Recursive hits (requiring database visit) are obviously slower than the queries that are answered from the *Data_Dictionary_Cache* (memory visit).

1.4   Redolog Buffers

Oracle records all transactions made against the database to enable the database to be recovered completely in the event of an unexpected database crash. Ultimately these changes will go to the *Redolog* files from where they are stored for future reference. But much before they are written to the *Redolog* files, all transactions made to the database are temporarily stored (cached) in the *Redolog* buffers of the *SGA*. The information in the *Redolog* buffers is written periodically (rather than continuously) to the *Redolog* files.

1.5   SMON, PMON, DBWR, LGWR

The process areas of the memory structure of Oracle constitute mainly four processes. They are *SMON, PMON, DBWR and LGWR*. The job of the first memory process, *SMON,* a short form for server monitor, is to assist in *Instance* (Oracle organisation) recovery. When the database is started, *SMON* comes into action if there was an *Instance* crash earlier. It helps in the recovery of the

16

Instance in the event of a crash, for example, due to file-read or off-line errors. It recovers transactions skipped during crash. If any temporary segment is blocked at the time of crash and it is no longer required, it is released. Further, if there are contiguous (one by the side of the other) areas of free space, *SMON* coalesces them into one chunk. All transactional objects are eliminated. There is one and only one *SMON* for a given *Instance*.

The next memory process, *PMON*, a short form for process monitor, is responsible for clearing any failed transactions. For example, if an *update* fails before *commit* due to a crash, all cache areas are cleared up, *Table* locks are released and other process resources are freed. It rollsback uncommited transactions.

There is one and only one *PMON* per *Instance*. If either *SMON* or *PMON* dies, the *Instance* also dies.

The next memory process known as *DBWR,* short form for dirty buffer writer, is important. It constantly watches two areas, the *Db_Buffer_*Cache and *Dictionary_Cache.* **The *DBWR*'s job is to write data from the buffer cache back to the database (disk) but it does not read data into the cache.** It is the job of the server process to read blocks from *Datafiles* and copy them into *SGA's Db_Buffer_Cache* and *Data_Dictionary_Cache.* Thus when a query is posed, the server process brings the data from the database into the *SGA*'s *Db_Buffer_Cache.* One copy of the data so retrieved from the database goes to *Rollback Segment.* The server process also writes in the *Data_Dictionary_Cache* the location of the records in the database from which the data was brought. This information is vital because after processing (like *update)* the data is to be returned to the original location from which it was brought. On updating the data, the changed data is first **copied** into *Redolog* buffers by the *DBWR.* The changed data in the *Db_Buffer_C*ache has to be returned to the database at the original location recorded in the *Data_Dictionary_Cache.* This transfer of changed data to database by the *DBWR* is not on a continuous basis. Instead, it is done periodically when the *Db_Block* buffer requires space to accommodate new incoming data. This implies that at a given time, the *Redolog* buffer contains a more up-to-date status of the database than the database itself.

This is simply because the *DBWR* may not have written the changed blocks back to the database since it was waiting for this writing. On *Commit*, the changed data in the *Redolog* buffer goes to the online *Redolog* files and the changed data in the *Db_Block* buffer has to go back to the database. If a *Rollback* command is given instead of *Commit*, the original data from the *Rollback Segment* is sent back to the database and the changed blocks in the *Redolog* buffer are purged out. The data retrieved from the database, irrespective of whether it was changed or not, has to return to the database.

If large queries are involved, multiple *DBWRs* will improve the performance. The *Db_Writer* parameter in the *Initn.Ora* file sets the number of *DBWRs* in the *Instance*. The job of *DBWR*, as the name suggests, is to write the changed blocks to the disk. The *DBWR* is responsible for providing sufficient space in the *Db_Block* buffer for new data.

If large amount of data is brought over into the *Db_Block* buffers for processing (*Update* etc.) and after processing, the data is kept uncommitted for too long, then it goes to *Rollback Segment* to be with the "before" image. This is done to make room in the *Db_Block* buffers for new data. So *Db_Block* buffer will not retain the data under process for too long. The *Rollback Segment* in this way operates like an extension of the *Db_Block* buffer.

The next memory process is *LGWR*, short form of log writer. As was mentioned earlier, in the *SGA*, the *Redolog* buffer cache accumulates the changed data. The job of *LGWR* is to write these changed data in batches from *Redolog* buffer cache to *Redolog* files. Thus the *Redolog* buffer cache entries are the most recent changed entries. While *DBWR*'s responsibility is to write changed data back to database files, *LGWR*'s is to write changed data cached in the *Redolog* buffer to *Redolog* files. This *LGWR* writing is done sequentially. It is important to note that *DBWR* accesses *Datafiles* in a random fashion. On *Commit*, although the changed blocks in *Db_Block* buffer are not written back to the disk, the changed data from *Redolog* buffers is written to *Redolog* files. *Commit* is considered complete, if and only if, the *Redolog* files are written to by the *LGWR*. *DBWR* writing into *Datafiles* is done

18

only when more space is needed in the *Db_Block* buffers to receive new information.

In the *Db_Block* buffer, even if there is no change to the data, i.e., records are not changed but only rolled back, the data must be rewritten back to the disk. The *DBWR* writes to the database are deferred to optimise the I/O traffic.

There is an additional memory process known as *CKPT* (check point, which is like a wake up alarm) available in the later versions of Oracle. It periodically prompts the *DBWR* to write all changed data blocks to the *Datafiles* and also prompts the *LGWR* to transfer *Redolog* buffer entries into *Redologs*.

1.6   Redolog Files

Next on list is the *Redolog* files. They hold records on all the modifying transactions that occur in the database. That means the information required to recover a database after a crash is in the *Redolog* files. After *Update* or *Delete*, a *Commit* is not considered operative (*Complete* message given) unless all modifications are written to *Redolog* files. In such situations, locks are held for the duration of the transaction to prevent destructive interaction from other processes or transactions. A *Commit* or *Rollback* releases the lock on the data.

Every database will have two or more *Redolog* files. If multiple *Redolog* files are provided, the entries to these are written in cyclic fashion. That is, to start with, the first *Redolog* file is written to. When it fills up, the second one is written to and so on and so forth until the last one fills. Then the first one is again written to (overwritten). But before overwriting the first *Redolog* file, all the information in it is copied into a tape or disk tape. Only then the overwriting takes place. This type of copying of the *Redolog* files to tape is known as archiving. If for some reason archiving is not possible (such as, tape not available), and overwriting has to be done, then the database comes to a standstill until archiving is provided. That is how the database ensures that no information is lost. Thus *Redolog* files contain such important information, and to provide redundancy, each of the multiple *Redolog* files is always provided with a duplicate (mirrored). As a matter of abundant caution, each *Redolog* file in the pair is located on a different disk. Even if one is lost, the other survives to provide the information required for recovery after a crash. Although *Redolog* files are related to the database, they are stored outside the database so that in event of a database crash, they are not lost.

1.7   Control File

A database's overall physical architecture is maintained by its *Control* files. These record control information about all the files within the database. They are used to maintain internal consistency and guide recovery operation. Since these *Control* files are critical to the database, multiple copies of these are stored in the database. *Control* files are *created* at the time of creation of the database. It was mentioned earlier that *DBWR* writes all changed datablocks from the *Db_Block* buffers to the database at *CKPT*. At the same time, datafile *Headers* and *Control* files are also entered to record these changes to the datablocks. Thus *Control* files maintain transaction control (*SCN*: System change number) and datafile information. During recovery, *SCN* is required. *Control* file records the occurrence of changes to any *Datafiles* and the exact time when the change took place (time stamp). The *Control* file also has complete information about the physical location of all *Datafiles* in the database.

An Oracle *Instance* is a methodology by which any *User* (customer) accesses the Oracle database.

There are many similarities between an *Instance* and the way, for example, a restaurant operates. First we will look at the restaurant for simplicity.

1.8   Restaurant Example

Let us take the example of an Indian restaurant. We shall see how the restaurant is run. We will then illustrate how the situation in an

Oracle *Instance* is similar to that in a restaurant. In a restaurant, Kitchen is the database. Several *Tablespaces* exist in this kitchen database (structure) as shown in Illustration 1.3.

Tablespace	Size	Data	No. of data
Container 1	10 L	Bread Slices	500
Container 2	20 L	Potato Curry	15 Kg
Container 3	15 L	Egg Plant Curry	15 Kg
Container 4	20 L	Lentils	10 L
Container 5	20 L	Yogurt	10 L
Container 6	10 L	Rice	15 Kg
Container 7	20 L	Chicken Curry	15 Kg
Container 8	1 L	Coconut Chutney	1 L
Container 9	3 L	Soup	2 L
Container 10	5 L	Appetizer	3 Kg
Container 11	6 L	Tea	5 L
Container 12	6 L	Coffee	5 L

Illustration 1.3 - Restaurant Structure

Let us look at the dining table. To start with, assume that there are several tables and chairs. All are clean and vacant since the restaurant was just opened.

1.9   Standard_Meal.Ora

Assume one single client (standalone - one *User* per *Instance*) arrives and is led by the hostess to a two-seater table. He occupies the chair (Login). The waiter takes the order as *Standard_Meal*. The waiter assembles the dining ware by looking at the file *Standard_Meal.Ora* as shown in Illustration 1.4. In a *Standard_Meal*, you get 6 Bread slices, Potato Curry 100 g, Egg Plant Curry 100 g, Lentils 100 ml, Yogurt 100 ml and Rice 100 g.

The vessels are filled with appropriate items and served to the *User*. Since the Meal was ordered as per the average requirement of a single *User*, he consumes it all. At the signal from the *User*,

21

the waiter brings the bill, collects the money and the *User* leaves (Logoff). The cleaner cleans the table and it is ready to receive another *User*. Here there is only one *User* at a time.

S No.	Parameter	No.	Required for
1	Num_Persons	1	
2.	Thali_Single	1	1
3.	Thali_Medium	0	2
4.	Thali_Large	0	6
5.	Large_Katori	0	
6.	Small_Katori	4	Four per person
7.	Spoon_Small	1	
8.	Water_Tumbler	1	
9.	Forks	0	
10.	Cup	0	
11	Serving Plate	0	

Illustration 1.4 - File Name: Standard_Meal.Ora for Standalone. (A Thali is a plate and a Katori is a bowl)

Instead of one, if you have a family of six people, the hostess will lead you to a six-seater table. (First step of the *Instance* determination). The waiter takes over from here. He solicits your order. Let us assume for your group of six, you order 33 Bread Slices, Potato Curry 500 g, Egg plant Curry 500 g, Lentils 500 ml, Yogurt 500 ml and Rice 500 g. Your family consists of a man, wife, grand-dad, grand-mom, boy and one girl. What you have ordered is a consolidated meal for all. Some may consume more of one item whereas others may consume more of a different item. It is meal for six based on average consumption. This type of ordering will cost much less than ala carte for each person. (consolidated requirement of six parallel *User*s in an *Instance*). So six people are going to share this *Instance* (*Shared Instance*).

1.10   Family_Meal.Ora

The waiter goes to the kitchen and assembles the dining ware for the *Family_Meal* as per the specifications in the file *Family_Meal.Ora* given in Illustration 1.5.

He fills the vessels with appropriate items ordered and serves them. Although the individual requirements may vary (e.g. man may eat more than the average number of bread slices, grand-dad and grand-mom may eat less), at the end, all the items get consumed. This is the principle of *Shared Instance*. The individual requirements of each *User* may slightly vary, but all the facilities offered get shared without much clash between the *Users*. Trouble comes only if any two members of the family (*Users*), demand a chunk much larger than the average of the same item in the *Family_Meal* and the quantity becomes insufficient. So in a *Shared Instance*, the requirements among individual *Users* should not be widely different for any resource.

S. No	Parameter No.	Required for	Remarks
1.	Num_Persons	6	
2.	Thali_Single	0	
3.	Thali_Medium	0	2
4.	Thali_Large	1	6
5.	Large_Katori	4	Curry1, Curry2, Lentils, Yogurt
6.	Small_Katori	24	Four per person
7.	Spoon_Small	6	
8.	Water_Tumbler	6	
9.	Forks	0	
10.	Cup	0	
11.	Serving Plate	6	

Illustration 1.5 - File Name: Family_Meal.Ora. (A Thali is a plate and a Katori is a bowl)

There is also another aspect to this *Shared Instance*. Since the order is for 33 bread slices, all are not served right in the

23

beginning, since space in the plate is not sufficient to accommodate all bread slices. The waiter serves 10 bread slices first and replenishes as and when they get consumed. If for some reason the production of bread slices in the kitchen gets slowed down, the process of eating on the table also gets slowed down.

The satisfaction of the customers depends largely on the correctness of the order placed. If too large a number of bread slices is ordered, many will be left unconsumed. If too little a quantity of curry is ordered, there will be a shortage. The order should be commensurate with the average requirements of the members of the set of *Users*.

Now let us see what happens in Oracle. A single *User* logs in. He opens the *Init.Ora* file (similar to a menu card) and names it *Init1.Ora* (order copy) to identify his requirements out of the database. The *User* has to tell Oracle his requirement (corresponding to the order of the customer in the restaurant). In the restaurant example there are only a few parameters. Oracle, which is capable of doing many tasks, in its later version has nearly 190 parameters. Fortunately, for an average *User*, most of the parameters are left at their default values and only a few parameters need to be specified. Even in a typical restaurant, there are default parameters. For example, water need not be ordered. It comes by default. If wrong parameters are chosen (unbalanced order in the restaurant), the performance of Oracle will be poor and *User* will not be satisfied with it. The choice of parameters is dictated by the way Oracle is used by the *User*. For example, if the *User* application is purely a decision support (*DSS*), i.e., it mostly is used to extract large information from the database by a single *User*, a large *RBS* is required assuming that the `Select` statement is used for a large number of records at a time. On the other hand, if the application needs frequent *updates (OLTP)*, smaller *Rollback Segment* is to be chosen in the *Init1.Ora*. This is because, *RBS* has to keep a copy of the set of records before *Update* till the data is *committed* or *rolled back*. Suppose, your *System* does not have a provision for an appropriate *RBS* for *OLTP*, then it will get overloaded. Similarly, if the application involves a large number of *Deletes/Updates*, then more *Redolog* files and *Archivelogs* have to be provided.

24

Thus, it is clear that allocation of different memory spaces in the *SGA* is very critical and the actual allocation depends on each application. Hence different types of *Instances* are to be configured for different types of applications. Otherwise a via-media approach of *Instance* may be designed to suit the requirements of a set of parallel *Users*.

1.11 Instance

In Oracle, using *Instance*, you can provide a plan of the configuration of several parameters for the shape of different memory structures etc. through which the database is accessed. Apriori, in order to efficiently get the job done through an *Instance*, you should first know what you want to do with the database after you access it. **There is no universal *Instance* which does all jobs with equal efficiency**. What all this means is, to have an equally efficient *Instance* for all jobs, you need an infinitely large memory. This can never be the case. The trick lies in managing the *Instance* to get the best results from the database with limited resources. This is like driving a car up or down a hill. The *Instance* used to go up the hill, (i.e., parameters are: low gear and foot on gas pedal) is different from the *Instance* used for going down the hill (i.e., slightly higher gear with foot on the brake). If you use the wrong parameters, the results of driving are disastrous. If you drive down hill in low gear, with foot on gas pedal, the car will crash. (*Instance* will crash).

So before you access a database, you must tell the *DBA* what you wish to do with the database. He should also be aware of the details of your application program so that he can assist you in getting better results. He can suggest minor changes in your software to manage with the limited resources set apart in that *Instance* in which your application fits best. Suppose you wish to *update* a large number of records, you may call all the records in one go, apply the change, and then *commit*. This requires an enoromous *RBS* space. Instead, you may call the records say 20 at a time, apply change and *commit* them. The requirement of *RBS* space in this case is considerably smaller. As was mentioned earlier, if you have an infinitely large memory area (which is not

25

practicable), you can *update* either way. However, there is an enoromous wastage of resources. Optimisation is the trick. The Restaurant *Instance* decides the optimisation to take care of all the parameters for the most efficient ordering of the food. Your *Instance* should be efficient and at the same time economical. It is similar to asking the waiter in the Restaurant to serve all the items of food in one go. This requires a very large table and the number of customers in the dining hall that can be served at a time will be reduced considerably. This is not required, because you do not eat all the items at the same time.

An *Instance*, therefore, is a plan of access of the Oracle database for a particular use. The parameters that you specify for that *Instance* determine the capabilities of that configuration of the Oracle database. Since the number of *Users* using the *Instance* is also a parameter, you can predetermine if one or more *Users* are going to use this *Instance* (table for one or six etc in the Restaurant). The same database can be accessed concurrently by several *Instances*. The parameter file that qualifies a given *Instance* is known as *Initn.Ora* file. ***Initn.Ora* file is not part of database.** Oracle processes do not write to it. Before Oracle starts, the *Init* file is read to organise Oracle. *Init1.Ora*, *Init2.Ora* etc. represent different *Instances*. Depending upon which *Instance* is more suitable for your requirement, you may access the database using that *Initn.Ora* file. To optimise the requirements of several concurrent *Users*, the *Instance* may be fashioned to satisfy the maximum number of *Users* within a group. Several *Instances*, as depicted in Illustration 1.6, may access the same database simultaneously.

Oracle database

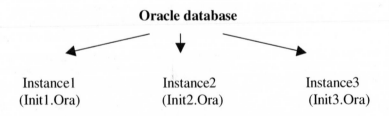

| Instance1 | Instance2 | Instance3 |
| (Init1.Ora) | (Init2.Ora) | (Init3.Ora) |

Illustration 1.6 - An Oracle Database Using Several Instances

An Oracle *Instance* should at least have

- One single datafile for its *System Tablespace*

- One single *Control* file (multiple copies)

- Two *Redolog* files

- One *Initn.Ora* file

- A minimum of four memory processes

In addition, the database should also have other *Tablespaces* for *User_Data, Temporary Space, RBS, Tools* etc.

It may be added that different authors give different definitions for database and *Instance*. Some authors prefer to separate database and *Instance* while others use them synonymously which gives rise to some confusion. These are distinctly different in a parallel server situation. If an Oracle parallel server is used, then the database consists of data on the disk stored in the operating *System* files whereas the *Instance* comprises *SGA* and the background processes. The database comprises database objects, data, *Tablespaces* including *Sytem, User* etc. The *Instance* comprises the *SGA* and its components and memory processes. Other authors combine the minimum requirements from both these parts and call it the *Instance*. Strictly speaking one does not exist without the other. Let us see what these items perform in an *Instance*.

The *System Tablespace* is the most important item of the *Instance*. Without *System Tablespace*, the *Instance* can neither be started nor sustained. This is so because it contains the *Data_Dictionary*, which in turn contains almost complete information about all aspects of database. If anybody accesses the *Data_Dictionary*, he gets a good idea about the database.

It may be added that *System Tablespace* should under no circumstances be allowed to contain *User*'s *Segment*s.

27

As mentioned earlier, when a *User* tries to access a given *Table* in the database using a particular *Instance* by, say the `Select` statement, it is the *Data_Dictionary* that determines whether such a *Table* exists, if so where it is located, and finally whether the *User* is duly authorised to `Select` the data from this *Table*. Hence *Data_Dictionary* acts like a faithful security officer who guards the data knowing fully well where the data exists and who has access authority to it. *Data_Dictionary* thus is an important source of information. If the *System Tablespace* goes offline, the *Instance* crashes.

The next item is the *Control* file. A database's overall physical architecture is maintained by its *Control* files. These record control information about the files within the database. The *Control* file also has complete information about the physical location of all *Datafiles* in the database. The *Control* files are used to maintain internal consistency and guide recovery operation. As will be seen later, during what is called a warm backup, the *Control* file is referred to. The *Control* file contains information about the current transaction state of all *Datafiles* in the database. Although *Control* file forms part of database, since it contains such sensitive information about the latest transaction state of the database, it is stored outside the database so that during unforeseen crashes, it is not lost. It is required during the recovery of database after the crash. Thus if the *Control* file is out of sync, the *Instance* will not start.

You may recall that Traveller's cheques issued by a bank are kept in one place and a copy of the serial numbers of all cheques is kept elsewhere. In case the cheques are lost, you may obtain replacement cheques by quoting their numbers from the list kept separately. If the traveller's cheques and the serial number list are kept together, they will be lost together and you can not get a replacement. That is, there is no recovery of the cheques. Due to their paramount importance, identical copies of all important files such as *Control* file are stored on different disks so that if one is lost, it can be copied from elsewhere.

Next on the list is *Initn.Ora* file. This completely defines all the parameters that decide the organisation of the *Instance*. Before start up, the *Initn.Ora* file of the particular *Instance* is first read. If during the use of an *Instance*, any parameters of *Initn.Ora* are to be modified for further use of the *Instance*, the file is opened, its relevant parameters are changed, the *Instance* is shut off and restarted. Then only the modified parameters become operational. Only the *DBA* is authorised to change the *Initn.Ora* parameters.

At least four memory processes are required to form an *Instance*. They are *SMON, PMON, DBWR, and LGWR*. Other processes may be augmented.

1.12 Database Creation

Suppose there is no database to start with. How do you *create* it? In this case, the *Instance* is initialised with *Nostartup Nomount* command as follows:

Start server manager by invocation of *SVRMGR* program. Connect to the *Instance* as connect internal. Next issue *Startup With Nomount*. At this point, there is no *Control* file. This starts a skeletal *Instance* process. Then issue *Create* database command. In this command one specifies maximum values for database structures like number of *Datafiles*/number of log files/number of *Instances* etc. These maximum parameters decide the fixed size of the *Control* file. If at a future date one wishes to change these sizes, the *Control* file has to be rebuilt. By this command, *System Tablespace, Redolog* file, *Control* file are built. In addition to these, to make the database usable, additional *Tablespaces, Rollback Segments, Redologs* should be added.

1.13 Database Startup

There are several steps to startup the database. In the above mode of database creation, the call was *Startup Nomount*. If the database already exists, the call is *Startup Open Mount*.

1.14 Database Shutdown

In order to shut down the database there are three approaches depending upon the contingency. For all the three, the first two steps are common.

Start the server manager (*SVRMGR*). Logon to database as connect internal or *User* with *DBA* or *SYSOPER* role. Then follow up with the shut down call in one of the three following commands. Suppose the database needs an urgent *shutdown* and there is no time to go through different steps of asking all *Users* to logoff, then use *Shut Down Abort* command. This will work if all other attempts to quickly *shutdown* the database fail. After such a shut down, the *Instance* needs recovery. There is another way that is *Immediate*. In this the database waits for pending transactions and shuts off *Users* and *Instance*. In such a shut down, the recovery of the *Instance* may be required. In the third and most natural shut down, the command is *Normal*. In this case, which is the slowest, the database waits for all *Users* to logoff whether they are idle or working. This type of shut down does not need recovery of *Instance*. **Even if one *User* logs on and goes home without logging off, the only way the database can be shutoff is by using *Immediate*.**

1.15 Alert Logs

The *Alert Log* file (*Alert_<SID> Log*) contains informational, warning and error messages related to Oracle core processes and. The *Alert Log* file must be checked once a day to ward off any impending trouble. If any database problem arises, first the *Alert Log* must be examined. Excessive waits for a checkpoint or waits that occur while *Redolog* files are written to *Archivelog* can be seen in *Alert Log*. Errors regarding background processes are seen in *Background_Dump_Dest* file.

Chapter 2   Tables

A database is a computer-based record keeping system. The nature
of information may be patient's records in a hospital or students'
records in a college. The data can be stored in more than one
database. A *Segment* is a collection of all occurrences of one type
of stored record. This can be a *Table* or an *Index*. For example,
Emp and *Dept* are *Table Segments*. These are fixed in size as
prescribed by the *User* when *created*. The size is defined in terms
of *Extents*. An *Extent,* for example, can have a size of 2048 bytes.
In the beginning, the *Table Segment Emp* may be assigned some
Extents (5 X 2048 bytes). When this space is used up by data, the
Table acquires additional *Extents* as prescribed by the *User* when
creating the *Table*. To start with, let us say, the *User* created 10
Tables, *T1*, *T2*,..., *T10*, of 5 *Extents* each. At some stage, the
Table T1 gets full and an additional 5 *Extents* are acquired by it.
These additional 5 *Extents* of *T1* are not contiguous with the
original 5 *Extents* of the *T1*. This is likely to create problems later.
When designing a new database, the *DBA* should have an idea of
the *Tablespaces* he has to provide for the *Users*. The *Users* in turn
have to estimate the *Tablespace* required for their use. The
estimation of size of the *Tables* by *Users* is neither exact nor
straightforward. This can be done as follows:

Choosing proper size for database objects such as *Tables* is very
important. To start with, the *User* has only limited information.
He knows the columns and their data lengths in the *Tables* he is
going to use. Assume that the data type is Varchar2. The actual
data that ocupy the column may not completely fill up all the
space provided. For example in Varchar2(10) if the actual data is
'SRIHARI', then only 7 out of 10 characters are occupied. Hence
some sample data are entered into the *Table* and the space
occupied is estimated. Therefrom, long term projections are made.
Based on such inputs from individual *Users*, the *DBA* makes the
overall space requirement for all the *Users* together. Let us see

how estimates for a *Table* size are made. If the data type is *Char* then all the assigned space is used up irrespective of the actual size of the data. That is in *Char*(10), even if the actual data is 7 characters long, the left over 3 characters space is not available for other use.

2.1   Table Size : VSIZE parameter

Let us assume that we have a *Table T1* with four columns as shown in Illustration 2.1.

Column 1	Varchar2(10)
Column 2	Varchar2(10)
Column 3	Varchar2(10)
Column 4	Varchar2(10)

Illustration 2.1 - Structure of Table T1

The upper limit of the Average Row Length (*Avg_Row_Length*) of this *Table* is 40. However, the actual data stored decides the *Avg_Row_Length* and it varies with changes in the data, either in their number or in their nature. Some records may occupy the entire length of 40 whereas others may occupy less. Suppose you have 20 records and you get an *Avg_Row_Length* based on these records. If you insert 20 more records, the new *Avg_Row_Length* may be more or less than the that for the first 20 records since each additional record has its own length. Hence one inserts sample data of some records into the empty *Table*. Then for all the *Tables* you own, you can obtain average row length (*Avg_Row_Length*). For *Table T1*, *Avg_Row_Length* is obtained by the following query.

```
SQL> Select Avg(nvl(VSIZE(Column1),0)) +
     Avg(nvl(VSIZE(Column2),0)) +
     Avg(nvl(VSIZE(Column3),0)) +
     Avg(nvl(VSIZE(Column4),0))
     Avg_Row_Length from User.T1;
```

The following SQL command gives the number of records in the *Table T1*.

```
SQL> Select Count(*) from User.T1;
```

The *Avg_Row_Length* can also be obtained without going through this SQL query. The Oracle database has provision to compute this and many other parameters pertaining to a given *Table* through automatic computation of *Statistics*. It may be noted that by the SQL command *Analyze*, the *Avg_Row_Length* can be obtained directly as will be seen later (Section 3.3 and Illustration 3.9).

The first query gives *Avg_Row_Length* based on the number of records, existing in the *Table T1*, given by the second query.

Since there are several rows in any *Table*, there should be a way to identify each row and differentiate it from other rows. This is because, suppose a record, undergoing *update*, has been sent to the *Db_Block_Buffer/RBS*. After *update*, the record has to be sent back to its original place. The record needs an identifier. This information is incorporated in *Row_Header*, unique to each row. This also occupies some space in the *Table T1*. The *Row_Header* information depends on whether the row has short (< 250 characters) or long (> 250 characters) columns.

Row_Header space per row = 3 + number of short columns + 3 * number of long columns.

Since *Row_Header* space is associated with each row, this is to be added to *Avg_Row_Length* to arrive at the total bytes required for each row.

Total bytes per row = (*Avg_Row_Length* + *Row_Header* space per row)

For *T1*, *Row_Header* per row = 3 + 4 = 7 bytes since all the 4 columns are short.

33

Assuming that there are R rows in the *Table T1*,

Total Bytes required for the *Table T1* containing R rows = R * (Total bytes/row)

This is the space needed to store the data in the *Table T1*. In addition to this space, there are some other overheads for space as follows:

Block_Header information is one more aspect required to identify the block in which the record is located. Earlier we have seen that every row should have an unique identifier called *Row_Header*. Now lets talk about the *Block_Header*. The record that was sent for *update*, has to be returned to its original location. There are many blocks each belonging to a *Datafiles*. In order to correctly send back the *updated* record, each block must have its own identifier. So *Block_Header* information also needs some space in the block. Estimating this is slightly tricky since determination of *Block_Header* size requires knowing how the data will be used. The *Block_Header* size has two parts to it, a *Fixed_Block_Header* size and a *Variable_Block_Header* size.

Fixed_Block_Header size = 57 + 23 * *Initrans*

Where the *Initrans* parameter indicates how the data is accessed. If only one transaction accesses the data in the datablock, the *Initrans* parameter is 1. If *m* transactions concurrently access the data in the datablock, then *Initrans* parameter = *m*. The default value is 1. This parameter is assigned a value while creating the *Table T1*. If the value of this parameter is kept lower than that is required, then the database temporarily uses the available free space in the datablock to support this requirement.

The second part of the *Block_Header* size i.e.,

Variable_Block_Header size = 4 + 2 * R where R is the number of rows/block.

In this expression, 4 denotes the space requirement of *Table Directory* (the *Table* segment to which the row belongs) whereas 2

34

denotes *Row Directory*. Thus we see that *Block_Header* size and data requirement are interrelated and hence it is tricky to estimate the *Table* space requirement. This is because, if there are more rows in the *Table T1*, i.e., R increases, the *Block_Header* size also increases (because it contains 2 * R term) and thereby leaving less space for the actual data. This brings in a small complication in the estimation of size for the *Table*. That is why one should calculate the free space available per block for the data. The block size is fixed for the *Operating System*. In our case it is 2048 bytes.

The *Db_Block_Size* parameter should never be changed unless the database is being recreated.

Assuming *Initrans* = 1,

Space available for data = [*Db_Block_Size* - *Fixed_Block_Header* size] = 2048 - 80 = 1968 bytes.

Out of the 1968 bytes, a provision of 20% is to be made for *Pctfree*. *Pctfree* space takes care of the future requirement of the space in the *Table* for *updates* of the data. *Pctfree* is understood as follows. Say, out of the R rows, a particular row is occupied by data of only 20 bytes and on *update*, the modified row occupies 30 bytes. Similarly suppose the original values are NULL and they are *update*d by some values. Where do you get this extra space from? *Pctfree* space is, therefore, provided for this contingency. Providing 20% for *Pctfree* is a thumb rule only.

Pctfree = 1968 * (20/100) = 393 bytes

Variable_Block_Header size = 4 + 2 * number of rows in the *Table* = 4 + 2R where R = Number of rows in *T1*.

Therefore, Available size of the block for data = (1968 - 393- 4- 2R).

We have already computed the space required per row as

Total bytes per row = (*Avg_Row_Length* + *Row_Header* space per row).

Thus the number of rows R = Available size for data /space required per row.

Let us take another example. In the case of our database, the *Table Tell_Det* has 20 columns, all short. It has *Count(*),* i.e., number of rows 79 for sample data. The *Avg_Row_Length* was 59.5 from the SQL *Analyze* query (Section 3.3). Total Block size is 2048 bytes.

Fixed block length is 57 + 23 * *Initrans.* Assuming *Initrans* = 1,

Fixed_Block_Header size = 80 Bytes. Available size = 2048 - 80 = 1968 bytes. Leaving 20% of this space equal to 393 bytes for *Pctfree*, and *Variable_Block_Header* size of 4 + 2R, the available size becomes 1968 - 393 - 4 -2R. In *Tell_Det, Row_Header* space per row = 3 + 20 since all are short columns. Space required per row = 59.5 + 23 = 82.5 bytes. Thus the number of rows R is given by

$$R = [1968 - 393 - 4 - 2R]/82.5 \text{ giving } R = 18.5 \text{ or } 18.$$

It should be made clear at this stage that no undue importance is to be given to these numbers. These calculations are at the most empirical and anything but rigorous. This is so because, if more data is added to the same *Table*, the *Avg_Row_Length* may change.

So in a given block of 2048 bytes, *Tell_Det* can accommodate 18 rows after providing for all overheads and *Pctfree* for future *updates*. This assumes that none of the columns in the *Table Tell_Det* is *indexed*. The final allocations of space in a block of 2048 bytes for *Tell_Det* are tabulated in Illustration 2.2.

R	Avg_Row _Length	Space for 18 rows of data	Block_ Header space	Row_Header for 18 rows	Pct free
18	59.5 bytes	1071 bytes	120 bytes	414 bytes	393 bytes

Illustration 2.2 -Table Tell_Det Allocations

It can be seen that out of 2048 bytes space in a block, only 1071 bytes are actually available for data. 120 bytes are taken up by the *Block_Header*. All the 18 rows put together need 414 bytes of space for *Row_Header* information. 393 bytes are set apart for *Pctfree*. If these overheads of space are not taken into consideration, we would have concluded that 2048 bytes can accommodate 2048/59.5 = 34 rows/block. In practice only 18 rows can be accommodated.

Since the data in these *Tables* is of Varchar2( ) type, the above computations of the number of data entries per block, R, remain unaltered even if the length of the data is changed to Varchar2(25). What if the data length is overdesigned to say Varchar2(50)? Let us assume that at first only a City name is inputted in this field. After making a large number of entries, it is decided that additional information of Street address and Zip Code are to be added. Since the data length provided in the design is sufficient, the column can accept this information. But there is a serious problem here. Much before *updating* a few of the R records in the block, the additional information takes up all the *Pctfree* space. Then for the rest of the records in the block, there is absolutely no space whatsoever to accommodate the additional information. This information will therefore spill over to another vacant block. That means, for all these records, whose additional information spills over to the other block, part of each record is in one block and the rest of the information in another block. This is known as *Chaining.* So to retrieve these records, the database has to search two blocks.

At any stage of database operation, how can one check whether the *Pctfree* provided is adequate or not? The answer lies here. After operation of the database, at some stage, count the number of records in the block by the command

```
SQL> Select Count(*) from T1;
```

Next, look at the *Row_Id* of the records. Here a brief explanation of *Row_Id* is warranted. This tag unequivocally identifies the physical location of a record in the *Table (Segment)*. It's format of 18 places is as shown in Illustration 2.3.

Block_Id	Sequence	File_Id	Nature
1-8	10-13	15-18	Places
00008791.	0001.	0003	Values

Illustration 2.3 - Format of Row_Id

The first 8 positions (00008791) in the *Row_Id* denote the *Block_Id*, i.e., the block in which the row resides. The second set of 4 numbers (0001) denote the sequence of the row in the particular block, i.e., in this case first row. The last 4 positions (0003) denote the *File_Id,* i.e., the *Segment* to which the row belongs. Here it is a number and its *Segment* name can be obtained from the view *Sys.dba_Extents* (Section 3.3.2 and Illustration 3.11).

The next step is to know the number of blocks in which these rows reside. It can be obtained through the following command:

```
SQL> Select Count
     (Distinct(Substr(Block_Id,1,8)||
     Substr(Row_Id,15,4)))
     from T1;
```

This gives the number of blocks in which all the rows of *T1* reside. Now *update* the records in *T1* in a manner that mimics future *updates*. Once again get *Count*, i.e., the number of blocks in which the records of *T1* reside after *update*. If the *Pctfree* is adequate, the number of blocks will remain the same before and after *update*. If the number increases after *update*, it implies that some of the *updated* rows have migrated to other block because the *Pctfree* is not adequate.

Row_Id helps in searching for data in a *Table*. *Row_Id* provides a path for search of the particular row. For example, look at the following query.

```
SQL> Select * from Tell_Hd where Row_Id =
     xxxx;
```

This will seek information by going to the *File_Id* first, then to the current block and finally to the current row. This way, the search path is minimised. *Indexing* is another efficient way to hasten the search by appropriate query.

2.2   Index

Indexing of columns in a *Table* enables fast search for data in the *Table*. Let us se how this takes place. Let us the take the example of *T1* (*Employee Table*) which has *Index* on three columns viz., City, State and Zipcode. The *Index* is created by the following command.

```
SQL> Create Index City-St-Zip-Indx
     On Employee(City, State, Zipcode)
     Initrans 2
     Maxtrans 100
     Tablespace Indexes
     Storage(Initial 4K
     Next 4K
     Pctincrease 0
     Minext 1
     Maxext 100);
```

This command creates an *Index* designated *City-St-Zip-Indx* on the *Table Employee* and the *Index* is stored in the *Tablespace Indexes* and is on three columns City, State and Zipcode. That means the data is arranged City-wise first, then State-wise and then Zipcode wise. For the query:

39

```
SQL> Select * from Employee
     where City = 'OMAHA' and
     State = 'NE';
```

the database will first search for the record in City and then in the State. Since the *indexing* is first on City and then on state, i.e., the *Index* sequence is same as the query sequence, it is efficient in search. An alternate query:

```
SQL> Select * from Employee
     where State = 'NE' and
     City = 'OMAHA';
```

will be less efficient in the search. If this query is to be searched fast, the *Index* sequence should be changed as follows;

```
SQL> Create Index St-City-Zip-Indx
     On Employee(State, City, Zipcode)
     Initrans 2
     Maxtrans 100
     Tablespace Indexes
     Storage(Initial 4K
     Next 4K
     Pctincrease 0
     Minext 1
     Maxext 100);
```

The meaning of all these parameters will become clear in the later chapters. Sometimes *indexing* becomes superfluous if the query is as follows, since the database has to go through the entire database.

```
SQL> Select * from Employee where
     City in ('NE','NJ','NY');
```

Take another *Table Personnel* in which employee data is stored and employeeNo (1-1000) is *indexed*. If the employeeNo is in sequence, query such as

```
SQL> Select * from Personnel
     where employeeNo = 111;
```

will be quickly searched. On the contrary, assume the employeeNo is not in sequence upto 1000. Then searching such a *Table* by the above query is very inefficient since the entire 1000 rows are to be searched. In such cases, to use the *Index* efficiently, the data is to be first sorted according to the employeeNo and then *indexed* on employeeNo. To sort the data, data has to be copied to a temporary location, sorted and brought back to the database in place of the original data (Section 9.2.1).

2.3 Primary/Foreign Key

In the *Tables*, the column or set of columns that define unequivocally a particular row is called the *Primary Key*. Once the *Primary Key* is created, the database *Indexes* this column automatically. Take the example of bank accounts of employees in a Bank Branch. The *Account Table* has the columns shown in Illustration 2.4.

AcctCode	AcctNo	Accttype	Holder's Name
1	1	Savings	B N Shah
2	1	Current	M N Ray
1	2	Savings	N V Lane
2	2	Current	M T Sarma

Illustration 2.4 - Details of Account Table

Luckily, the holder'name in this small *Table* can be a *Primary Key*. A cursory look at any telephone book tells you that often two people have the same lastname as well as initials and hence it is not safe to pick the holder's name as the *Primary Key*.

41

This is being aptly reflected for hundreds of years in the Hindu wedding rituals. Every year, Lord Rama's wedding is performed all over the state of Andhra Pradesh in India. During that time the priest recites what is called the *Pravara*. This *Pravara* recitation has been practiced for hundreds of years in all Hindu weddings in that state and continues even today. The couples may not realise this due to loud background music at the time of this recitation in Sanskrit. Instead of pronouncing that LORD RAMA (groom's name) hereby marries SITA (Bride's name), the priest announces:

Know all these men by these presents that

King Yayati's great-great-grandson, King Nabhagudu's great-grandson, King Ajudu's grandson and King Dasaradha's son LORD SRI RAMA

<u>hereby weds</u>

King Maha Romudu's great-great-granddaughter, King Swarna Romudu's great-granddaughter, King Hrasva Romudu's granddaughter and King Janaka's daughter SITA.

Thus from these ancient times it was realised that any person in this world can be uniquely identified if you quote names of father/grandfather/great-grandfather and great-great-grandfather along with the name of the person. Thus the *Primary Key* (person, father, grandfather, great-grandfather, great-great grandfather) is considered adequate for sure identification.

Coming back to the Bank accounts, the column Acctcode can not by itself be the *Primary Key* because there are two rows with identical Acctcodes. Similarly AcctNo can not be the *Primary Key*. However, a combination of Acctcode and AcctNo uniquely defines a given row in that *Table*. Hence the *Primary Key* (Acctcode, AcctNo) is acceptable. Similarly *Primary Key* (AcctNo, Accttype) is also acceptable.

2.4   Sizing Indexes (Non-clustered Tables)

So far we assumed that in the *Table T1*, there are no *Indexes*. Let us consider another *Table T2* with three columns with Column1 and Column2 *indexed*. That is, they constitute *Primary Key*, Pk (Column1, Column2)   and Column3 is not *indexed*. All the Columns have Varchar2(10) length. There is no other *Table* to which *Table T2* is related by any *Foreign Key*. That means there is no referencing of the *Primary Key*. To size such a situation, first obtain the *Average_Index_Entry_Length* of the *indexed* Columns 1 and 2 as follows:

```
SQL> Select Avg (nvl(VSIZE(Column1),0)) +
     Avg(nvl(VSIZE(Column2),0))
     Avg_Index_Entry_Length
     from T1;
```

In addition to the above space requirement, each *Index* entry has *Row_Header* information.

Row_Header space/*Index* Entry =

3 + Number of short columns + 3 * (Number of long columns)

Total bytes/entry = *Avg_Index_Entry_Length* + *Row_Header* space/entry. Assume, the *Avg_Index_Entry_Length* = 18 bytes from the above query. *Row_Header* space = 3 + 2 = 5 bytes since only two columns are *indexed*. Total bytes/entry = 18 + 5 = 23 bytes. For *Indexes*, the value of *Initrans* parameter >= 2. Taking the minimum, *Fixed_Block_Header* space =   57 + 2 * 23 = 103 bytes, the available space per block for data = 2048 - 103 = 1945 bytes. In the *Index* case, *Pctfree* portion is 5%, i.e., 1945 * 5/100 = 97 bytes. Thus we are left with 1945 - 97 = 1848 bytes per block for data. However, there is another overhead for *Block_Header,* namely *Variable_Block_Header*, which is equal to (4 + 2R) where R is the number of entries per block. This leaves (1848 - 4 - 2R) bytes for data. The number of bytes per entry was arrived at above as 23. To play it safe an additional 5% overhead to this is added. This makes the number of bytes per entry = 23 + 23 * 5/100 = 24

In *Table T2*, where two of the three columns are *indexed*, the number of entries R = (1848 - 4 - 2R)/24 giving R = 70. Thus in this case, 70 entries can be there in a block of 2048 bytes after appropriations, as indicated in Illustration 2.5.

Block Size	Header Space	Pctfree	Data	Num_Rows
2048 bytes	103+144 bytes	97 bytes	1731 bytes	70

Illustration 2.5 - Allocation of Space in the Block

Let us assume that there are actually 70 rows in *T2*. The *Index* information for *T2* needs one block.

2.5   Sizing Indexes (Clustered Tables)

In *Clustered Key* situations, there is a *Primary Key* in *Table T1* and it is referenced by the same Column as *Foreign Key* in *Table T2*. An example would be, Deptno in *Emp Table* and Deptno in *Dept Table*. Such *Clustered Table* data are stored in a slightly different way compared to the *Unclustered Table* data. This will help in accessing the data if the manipulation involves reference to both the *Tables*. **This advantage will be lost if manipulation involves reference to only one of the two *Tables*.** The column Deptno is called the *Cluster Key*. Once this *Cluster Key* is *created*, data can be entered into the *Cluster* blocks and their associated *Table* columns.

Assume that *T1* has three columns of Varchar2(10) and *T2* has two columns, one of Varchar2(5) and the other of Varchar2(10). Assume that Column3 of *T1* and Column2 of *T2* are *Cluster Keys*. In this case, *Initrans* = 2 and there are two overheads to the *Block_Header* size. One is the *Table Directory* and the other *Row Directory*. The former is given by (4*N + 1) where N is the number of *Tables* in the *Cluster* (here N = 2) and the latter is equal to 2 bytes/row in a block. If there are R rows in a block, 2R is the space needed for *Row Directory*.

44

As usual, *Block_Size* = 2048 bytes.

Block_Header Size = *Fixed_ Block_Header* Size +

Variable_Block_Header Size.

$$= 57 + 23 * Initrans + (4N + 1) + 2R$$

$$= 57 + 23 * 2 + (4 * 2 + 1) + 2R$$

$$= 112 + 2R$$

Available space for data per block   = 2048 - (112 + 2R) = (1936 - 2R)

Now the *Row_Header* requirement has to be arrived at. We need to compute the *Avg_Row_Length* of all the columns other than the *Cluster Key* in both the *Table*s. In the first *Table T1*,

```
SQL> Select Avg(nvl(VSIZE(Column1,0)) +
     Avg(nvl(VSIZE(Column2),0))
     Avg_Row_Length1
     from T1;
```

In the second *Table T2*,

```
SQL> Select Avg(nvl(VSIZE(Column1),0))
     Avg_Row_Length2 from T2;
```

Thus *Non_clustered Key* columns are used in this computation of *Avg_Row_Length*.

Since so far the *Avg_Row_Length* obtained above does not include space required for the *Cluster Key* column (Column3 of *T1* and Column2 of *T2*), let us examine the requirements of the *Cluster Key*.

Row length/row = *Row_Header* space/row + Number of short columns + 3 * number of long columns + *Avg_Row_Lengths* for *T1(T2)*.

From the result of SQL command of *Analyze*, assume we obtained 20 and 3 as *Avg_Row_Length* of *T1* and *T2*.

Row_Header space per row in *Clustered Table* = 4 bytes

Row length/row for *T1* = 4 + 2 + 20 = 26 bytes

Row length/row for *T2* = 4 + 1 + 3 = 8 bytes

The minimum acceptable for row length for *Cluster* is 10 bytes. So for *T2*, the row length/row = 10 bytes

The number of rows in *T1* and *T2* are not the same. These are obtained from the sample data in the *Tables*.

```
SQL> Select Count(*)Rows_Per_Key,
     Count(Distinct(Columname)) DISTCOL,
     DISTCOL/Rows_Per_Key
     from T1(and T2):
```

We get 30 for *Row_Per_Key* for *T1* and 1 *Row_Per_Key* for *T2*. Next the size of the *Cluster Key* column is to be determined.

```
SQL> Select Avg(nvl(VSIZE(ClusterColumn),0))
     Avg_Key_Length from T1;
```

Assume we obtained a value of 5 bytes for the *Avg_Key_Length* from this query. It is the same for *T2* also.

Row length = [*Rows_Per_Key* in *T1* * *Avg_Row_Length1*] +

[*Rows_Per_Key* in *T2* * *Avg_Row_Length2*] +

[*Cluster_Key_Header*] + [Column Length of *Cluster Key*] +

[*Avg_Length_Cluster Key*] +

2 * [Rows/*Cluster Key* in *T1* + Rows/per *Cluster Key* in *T2*]

The *Cluster_Key_ Header* is 19 bytes.

Row length/*Cluster Key* = (30 * 26) + (1 * 10) + 19 +

$$10 + 5 + (2 * (30 + 1))$$

$$= 780 + 10 + 19 + 10 + 5 + 62$$

$$= 886 \text{ bytes} = 900 \text{ bytes/}Cluster\ Key$$

Available Space for data/block = (1936 - 2R)

The number of *Cluster Keys* entries/block = (Available space)/ (Row length + 2 * Rows per key) = ((1936 - 2R)/ (900 + 2 * 30)) which is equal to R. Solving for R (= 1936/962) gives the number of *Cluster Key* entries/block as 2. Thus in any given block there will be only two entries of *Cluster Keys*.

Let us assume that the *Tables* are *Emp* and *Dept*. From the above it is clear that two values of Deptno from *Dept Table* will occupy one block. If the *Dept Table* has four values, 10, 20, 30 and 40 of Deptno, then we need two blocks for the data of *Emp* and *Dept*.

If we do not know the number of entries in *Dept*, query the *Table* as follows:

```
SQL> Select Count(Distinct(Column))Z
     from Dept;
```

Then Z/2 gives the number of blocks required for the data.

It may be noted here that (a) *Indexes* can not be *created* on *Views* and (b) *Dropping* an *Index* in a *Table* does not affect the data.

Chapter 3 DBA Routine Monitoring

There is a need to monitor databases periodically after continuous operation for a while. This is similar to what one does in domestic spending. When a man sets up a family for the first time, he does not know *apriori* what his family maintenance costs would be. So he uses educated guesses and appropriates different amounts under different heads for food, rent, water, car installment, entertainment etc. At the end of the month, he reviews the situation based on actual expenses under different heads and may make some changes in the appropriations in the next month. After a few months, he arrives at the most optimum appropriation. If and only if, some major additional expense arises, such as that due to arrival of a child in the family, he needs to change the appropriations. Similar situation exists in a database. Hence there is a need to look at the appropriations periodically for different *Tablespaces* in the database.

The monitoring schedule typically comprises the following:

- Resource Utilisation

- Preventive Measures

- Security Checks

Let us see what each one of these three does.

3.1   Resource Utilisation

In the first place, when a database is created, one chooses several parameters in the *Initn.Ora* file to allocate some of the resources such as memory spaces from the database. Besides, some spaces are provided for *Tablespaces* such as *System*, *RBS*, *User_Data* etc. At some stage of operation of the database, we have to review these allocations to see the status of these allocations and also to see if these spaces are being adequate or not being utilised for the purpose for which they were kept apart. This type of monitoring at appropriate intervals of time is needed to remove allocations that are no longer required and provide additional space for new *Users* or augmenting old *Users*, if needed. This will also help in following up the growth of the database and thereby enabling the *DBA* to forecast the future requirements for disk space. We have to devise SQL queries on different views of the database to extract this information. Scripts for most of these SQL statements are readily available.

3.1.1 Tablespace: Allocated and Used

To start with, one has to first find out the amounts of spaces allocated for all the *Tablespaces* in the database. In order to query the database, the *DBA* creates various *Views* because the database can not be queried directly. Whoever has *DBA* privileges can query these *Views*. For example, to obtain the above information, two *Views* are to be created. They are *Ts_Alloc, Ts_Used*. If these *Views* are to be made accessible to all *Users*, public synonyms for these *Views* are to be created.

3.1.2 View Creation

The *View Dba_Data_Files* (Section 4.5) gives information about *Ts_Alloc*.

```
SQL> Create or Replace View Ts_Alloc
     as  Select  Tablespace_name,  Sum(bytes)
     Bytes_Alloc
     from Dba_Data_Files;
```

View Created

49

The *View Sys.dba_Extents* (Section 3.3.2) gives the information about the *Ts_Used*.

```
SQL> Create or Replace View Ts_Used
     as Select Tablespace_Name, Sum(bytes)
     Bytes_Used from Sys.dba_Extents group
     by Tablespace_Name;
```

View Created

3.1.3   Synonym Creation

```
SQL> Create Public Synonym Ts_Alloc for
     Ts_Alloc;
```

Synonym Created

```
SQL> Create Public Synonym Ts_Used for
     Ts_Used;
```

Synonym Created

Every User can access these two *Views* without *grant* of any special *Privilege*. In the database I dealt with, some of the rows returned from querying these two *Views* are given in Illustration 3.1

From these results it is clear that the *Tablespace RBS* was allocated 4.09 MB and only 3.14 MB was utilised. It is similar with the other two *Tablespaces*. Such inputs tell us how well the spaces allocated are being used. In addition, they help in forecasting the future requirements.

Ts_Name	Bytes_Alloc
RBS	4,096,000
System	10,485,760
User_Data	3,145,728

Ts_Name	Bytes_Used
RBS	3,145,728
System	7,286,784
User_Data	92,160

Illustration 3.1 - Typical Bytes Allocated and Used in My Database

3.1.4　Freespace

Sometimes, you encounter a different situation. As you go on adding data to an existing *Segment* such as a *Table* in a *Tablespace*, the space in the *Segment* gets filled up. If you try to add additional *Extents* to an existing *Segment*, you may fail. Then you have to determine how much *Freespace* is available in the *Tablespace* by querying the database as follows:

- *Ts_Alloc*


```
SQL> Select * from Ts_Alloc;
```


This returned 4 rows in another database as detailed in Illustration 3.2.

Tablespace_Name	MB
RBS_Data	419.43
Org_Name	1572.86
System	419.43
User_Data	83.88

Illustration 3.2 - Allocated Bytes in Another Database

- *Ts_Used*

```
SQL> Select * from Ts_Used;
```

This gave 4 rows in the same database as given in Illustration 3.3.

```
SQL> Select a.Ts_Name, a.Bytes
     Used_Mbytes, b.Bytes Alloc_Mbytes
     (b.Bytes - a.Bytes)/1000000
     Free_Mbytes
     from Ts_Used a, Ts_Alloc b
     where a.Ts_Name = b.Ts_Name;
```

For my database, the result of the above query is shown in Illustration 3.4.

Tablespace_Name	MB
RBS_Data	389.81
Org_Name	440.42
System	382.62
User_Data	32.46

Illustration 3.3 - Used Bytes in Another Database

Ts_ Name	Used_ Mbytes	Alloc_ Mbytes	Free_ Mbytes
RBS	389.81	419.43	29.62
Org_Name	440.42	1572.86	1132.44
System	382.62	419.43	36.81
User_Data	32.46	83.88	51.42

Illustration 3.4 - Free Bytes in Different Tablespaces

If enough *Freespace* is not available, *Alter Tablespace* command can be issued to add space as follows:

```
SQL> Alter Tablespace User_Data
     add datafile
     '/User1/Oracle/Prod/Users02.dbf'
     size 100 M;
```

3.2   Fragmentation

As more data gets added to the *Segments* in the *Tablespace*, the *Segments* get filled up and you can allot additional *Extents*. A situation may arise such that although you may have lot of *Freespace* in the *Tablespace*, still you fail to add new *Extents* to an existing *Segment.* This is because there is another way the available *Freespace* can effectively get reduced. As *deletes* are performed on different *Segments* in the *Tablespace*, small chunks of *Freespace* are being created therein. Take the situation as follows: Let us assume that in a given *Tablespace*, there are three *Segments* S1, S2 and S3 with *Freespace* designated by FS at a given time as given in Illustration 3.5A.

S1	S2	S2	S3	S1	S1	FS1	FS2

Illustration 3.5A - Freespace at a Given Time of Database Operation

53

After several days of operation of the database which included *deletes/updates*, the situation would have changed to that given in Illustration 3.5B.

S1	FS3	FS4	S3	S1	S1	FS1	FS2

Illustration 3.5B - Freespace After Sometime of Database Operation

That means *Segment* S2 was *deleted* creating two contiguous *Freespaces* (FS3 and FS4). But the next *Freespaces* (FS1 and FS2) are not contiguous with this *Freespace*, because *Segments* S3 and S1 are in between the two *Freespaces*. So in course of time, because of *deletes*, several small chunks of such *Freespace* are *created* and each of these is not large enough to be useful. However, they amount to a considerable percent of the total free *Tablespace* with no utility. This is called *Fragmentation* of space. *Fragmentation* can take place even within a *Segment* just like within a *Tablespace*. Once this occurs, attempts to create a new *Table* or add additional *Extents* to an existing *Table* fail, since any of these chunks is not large enough by itself. Under these circumstances, you have to remedy the situation to bring all these chunks together (coalesce them into one large chunk of space), the process known as *Defragmentation*. In the first place, you must know if *Fragmentation* is taking place at all and if so, is it sufficiently high enough as to warrant *Defragmentation*. To learn about the severity of *Fragmentation*, you have to query the database and obtain the relevant information as follows:

3.2.1 Contig_Space

```
SQL> Select * from Contig_Space;
```

54

This query is used to find out where contiguous *Freespace* exists in the database. For our database it gives 42 rows. One of these is given in Illustration 3.6.

Ts_ Name	File _Id	Block _Id	Starting File_Id	Starting Block_ Id	Num of Blocks	Bytes
Org_ Name	6	287	6	287	10	20480

Illustration 3.6 - Contiguous Freespace in the Tablespace

That means in *Org_Name Tablespace*, where Block_Id = 287 and in the *Segment* with *File_Id* = 6, there are 10 contiguous free blocks available.

Look at the Illustration 3.4. The *Tablespace, User_Data*, has 51.42 MB *Freespace*. You still fail to create new *Extents* of 50 MB for the new *Tables* in *User_Data*. Then you have to find out if the *Freespace* of 51 MB in *User_Data* is scattered so that there is no single chunk of 50 MB in contiguous blocks. To know this, look at the following *View* of the database:

3.2.2 Dba_Free_Space

The columns in this *View* are:

Ts_Name/File_Id/Block_Id/Bytes/Blocks/ Relative_Fno. In our database, the following query shows where *Freespace* exists in the *Tablespaces*.

```
SQL> Select * from Dba_Free_Space;
```

In our database, 44 rows were returned of which three are given in Illustration 3.7.

Ts_ Name	File _Id	Block _Id	Bytes	Blocks	Rel FNo
User_ Data	5	152	49,336,320	24,090	5
System	6	21997	1,12,238,592	54,804	6
User_ Data	2	1387	1,433,600	70	2

Illustration 3.7 - Freespace in Tablespaces

However, in the above *View*, Owners' name is not given. If we are interested in the name of the owner also, we have to couple the above query with that on another *View, Dba_Extents* as follows:

```
SQL> Select
     'Free_Space' Owner,
     '           ' Object,
     File_Id,
     Block_Id,
     Blocks
     from Dba_Free_Space
     where Tablespace_Name = 'User_Data'
     UNION
     Select
     Substr(Owner,1,20),
     Substr(Segment_Name,1,32),
     File_Id,
     Block_Id,
     Blocks
     from Dba_Extents
     where Tablespace_Name = 'User_Data'
     Order by 3,4;
```

The output for our database from this union is shown in Illustration 3.8.

Owner	File_Id	Block_Id	Blocks
Freespace	5	152	24,090
Freespace	2	1337	10
Freespace	2	1377	5
Freespace	2	1387	70

Illustration 3.8 - Freespace in Different Blocks of the Database

In the Illustration 3.7, in the *User_Data Tablespace*, a chunk of 1.4 MB out of 50.7 MB *Freespace* is not contiguous with the 49.3 MB chunk. So attempts to add 50 MB *Extents* to the *Segments* in the *User_Data Tablespace* failed. To know whether *Fragmentation* in a *Segment* has taken place or not, one can run the following query.

```
SQL> Select Owner, Segment_Name,
     Segment_Type,
     Sum(bytes) Tot_Bytes, Count(*) Frags
     from Sys.dba_Extents
     where Owner NOT IN ('SYS','SYSTEM')
     Having Count(*) > 1
     Group by Owner, Segment_Name,
     Segment_Type
     Order by Frags Desc;
```

The above query was run for my database under two conditions :

• Condition 1:

```
where Owner = 'URKRAO'
```

Removed the clause (Having Count(*) > 1). Removed the last two clauses(Group by) and (Order by).

The result was: 56 rows selected all with **Count(*) = 1**. So in my database, there are 56 objects (*Tables/Indexes* together) and none of then has **Count(*) > 1**. This implies that none of these *Tables/Indexes* has *Fragmentation*.

- Condition 2:

```
where Owner = 'URKRAO'
Having Count(*) > 1.
```

Removed the two clauses (Group by) and (Order by). The result was: No rows selected. Again it confirms that none of the 56 *Tables/ Indexes* have *Frags*.

Let us try to understand how *Fragmentation* is implied in the above query output. For a *Table T1*, when we created it in the beginning, we provided *Extent* E1 of 10 MB. Then we also provided for another *Table T2* with *Extent* E2 of 20 MB. Subsequently, so much data was put into *T1* that it filled up the 10 MB space. We provided additional 10 MB in *Extent* E3. E1, E2 and E3 are contiguous. Now for some reason, we deleted *T2*, i.e., *Extent* E2 of 20 MB is *Freespace*. But *T1* has two *Extents* E1 and E3 which are separated from each other by an empty *Freespace* E2. Now If we run the above query for *T1* we get the output with Totbytes = 20 MB and Frag [Count(*)] = 2, i.e., *T1* has two *Extents* separated from each other. We then understand that *T1* is *fragmented*.

Similarly, the above query can be used to obtain information about *Fragmentation* of *Indexes* by substituting Segment_Type = 'Index' and Segment_Name = 'co8745'. It may be added here that any *Tablespace* or *Table* can be *defragmented* by using the Oracle Utilities *Export/Import* (Section 7.4).

3.3   Other Useful Views

In addition to the above, there are several other *Views* in the database that are useful for *Users*. Some of the more important ones are given below. Sample outputs are also provided for illustration.

3.3.1 Dba_Tables

The following query gives complete information about all the *Tables* in the database.

SQL> Select * from Dba_Tables;

This is probably one of the largest of all *Tables* with 37 columns. In view of the wealth of information it provides, it is reproduced here with one row out of 36 rows obtained in our database with Owner = "URKRao".

It may be noted that in Illustration 3.9 there are a few columns of interest to us. They are: *Last_Analysed, Num_Rows, Avg_Row_Length, Chain_Count* etc. These parameters are to be *updated* periodically by computing internally. There is a command, *Analyze*, to initiate this computation as follows:

In our database, we login as "URKRao" and enter the password.

- Execute the following *Analyze* command which fills the *Table* called *Chained_Row:*

  ```
  > Analyze Table Employee List Chained
    Rows;
  ```

- *Create* a temporary *Table* called *Chained_Employee* as follows to store *Chained_Rows:*

  ```
  > Create Table Chained_Employee as
    Select * from Employee where
    Row_Id IN
    (Select Head_Rowid from
    Chained_Rows);
  ```

1	2	3	4	5	6
Owner	Table_ Name	Ts_Name	Cluster _Name	IOT _Name	Pct free
URKRao	Tell_Hd	Org_Name			10

7	8	9	10	11	12
Pct used	Initrans	Max_ Trans	Initial_Ext	Next_Ext	Min_ Ext
40	1	255	10240	01240	1

13	14	15	16	17	18
Max_ Ext	Pct_ Inc	Free_ Lists	Free_ List_Gp	Logging	Back _Up
121	50	1	1	Yes	No

19	20	21	22	23	24
Num_ Rows	Blocks	Empty_ Blocks	Avg_ Space	Chain_ cnt	Avg_Row_ Len
27	1	3	766	0	42

25	26	27	28	29	30
Avg_Space _Free_ Blocks	Num_ Freelist_ Blocks	Deg- ree	Inst- ance	Cache	Table_ Lock
766	1	1	1	N	Enabled

31	32	33	34	35	36
Sample _Size	Last_ Analyzed	Parti- tioned	Tot_Type	Temp- orary	Nested
0	05-MAR- 1999	NO		N	NO

37
Buffer_Pool
Default

Illustration 3.9 - One Typical Row from Dba_Tables

- Delete the *Chained_Rows* from the *Table Employee*:

  ```
  > Delete from Employee where Row_Id IN
  (Select Head_Rowid
  from Chained_Rows);
  ```

- Insert the rows back into the *Table Employee:*

  ```
  > Insert into Employee
  Select * from Chained_Employee;
  ```

- Drop the temporary *Table Chained_Employee;*

  ```
  > Drop Table Chained_Employee;
  ```

The columns of *Table Chained_Rows* are described in Illustration 3.10.

Column	Description
Table_Name	Table name
Owner_Name	Table owner
Cluster_Name	Cluster name, if exists
Head_Rowid	Row_Id of chained row
Timestamp	Date and time of Analyze command execution

Illustration 3.10 - Chained_Rows Table Description

```
SQL> Analyze Table URKRao.Tell_Det
     compute statistics;
```

This will commence computation of statistics on the *Table Tell_Det* owned by "URKRao". Now to obtain the above information, query *Dba_Tables* **where Table_Name =**

61

`'Tell_Det'`. The result will be upgraded as on this date of query (Last_Analyzed column).

Notice column number 23, *Chain_Count* of the above *Table*. As was mentioned earlier, if the *Pctfree* is kept low, *updating* of a few records may consume all the available free space. Further *updating* results in *Chaining* of records (Section 2.1). This means that due to lack of space in the block, *updating* by additional information of each record spills over into next vacant block. The database has to search different blocks for each of such records. The above *Analyze* command gives the *Count* of such *Chained records* under column 23.

3.3.2   Sys.dba_Extents

Here is another *View* to look at your own *Tables* in the database.

```
> Select * from Sys.dba_Extents
  where owner = 'URKRAO' and
  Segment_Type = 'Table';
```

In my database, this command gives 36 rows (i.e., 36 *Tables*). One of them is as given in Illustration 3.11.

Owner	URKRao
Segment_Name	Tell_Det
Partition Segment_Type	Table
Ts_Name	User_Data
Extent_Id	0
File_Id	0
Block_Id	20042
Bytes	20480
Blocks	10
Relative_Fno	6

Illustration 3.11 - Typical Output from Sys.dba_Extents for Tables

62

Sys.dba_Extents View can also be queried for information on *Index* by substituting *Segment_Name = 'Index'* in the above query. Some of the entries obtained therefrom for *Indexes* of my data are given in Illustration 3.12.

Segment Name	Bytes
Sys-coo6278	20480
Sys-coo6284	10240
Pk-AccnoCo	10240

Illustration 3.12 - Output from Sys.dba_Extents for Index

If the *System Tablespace* shows *Fragmentation* and excessive *I/O* traffic, it indicates that a *User's Temporary Tablespace* assignment has been set to *System*.

Chapter 4   Preventive Measures

It was mentioned earlier that in our monthly expenditure, as time passes, we have to change the appropriations under different heads due either to the changed circumstances or due to faulty appropriations in the first place. For example, if we appropriated 10% of the total take home salary for food and at the end of the month we found that the actual expenditure far exceeded this allocation, in the next month we have to increase this from 10% to some higher value. We might have spent less than the appropriated amount in the case of some other item. We then reduce its appropriation in the following month. This leads to tuning of expenditure. Many Governments resort to this type of remedial action. They find that for some social purposes the expenditure goes beyond the budgeted amount. They may then reduce revenue expenditure or alternatively find some new resources of income to take on this additional expense. This is a mid-course correction to the budget, forecast at the beginning of the year. This is exactly what one does in database preventive measures. If some allocations for a given *Tablespace* are not adequate, it is either augmented by additional memory or some other allocation is cut down and added where needed. But before we do that, we should know where the correction needs to be applied.

In order to look at the health of the database, Oracle provides means for collection of *Statistics* while the database is being transacted by *Users*. This becomes necessary if some problems like slowing down of Oracle or sometimes crashing of Oracle occurs. Much before that happens, it is advisable to periodically look at the health of the database just as they do in preventive medicine. Doctors for example, give vaccinations to children to prevent development of some diseases at a later date. In Oracle, collection of *Statistics* on the database is the means to foresee trouble spots ahead of time. Oracle can continuously update a set of internal *Statistics*, which are stored in what are called *Tracking*

Tables. These *Statistics* are reset every time the database is shut down and restarted. It may be noted here that conclusions drawn from the *Statistics* collected in a time interval during day time are different from the conclusions drawn based on *Statistics* collected in the same time interval during night time (silent hours). This is because the type of transactions performed during day are likely to be different from the type of transactions performed during night time. The *Statistics* are not automatically collected in Oracle. For example, to collect the relevant *Statistics* pertaining to *Db_Block Statistics*, open *Initn.Ora* file and set the *Db_Block_Lru_Statistics* parameter to 'TRUE'. Then *Shutdown* the database, restart the *Instance,* and the collection of *Statistics* of *Db_Block_Lru* will commence. Continue till t = t. In between, the database should not be *Shutdown.* If it is shutoff, the *Statistics* will be reset. At the end of t = t, go back to *Initn.Ora* and reset the *Db_Block_Lru_Statistics* parameter to 'FALSE'. Otherwise, collection of *Statistics* will continue and it will slow down the database performance.

Oracle 7 provides two scripts *UTLBSTAT.SQL* and *UTLESTAT.SQL* located in the *Admin* subdirectory of Oracle.Home directory. The first script *creates* a set of empty *Tables* and populates them with *Statistics* at the beginning (B), at t = 0. The second script runs later at End time (E), at t = t, and *creates* a set of *Tables* based on the *Statistics* in the database at that time and finally generates a report known as *Report.txt* that lists changes in the *Statistics* during the interval between the two run times (t = 0) and (t = t) of the two scripts. There is a slight complication here. If the *Tables UTLBSTAT* and *UTLESTAT* are located in the database of which *Statistics* are being monitored, then the results will get tarnished by the *Statistics* of the *Tables* generated by *UTLBSTAT* and *UTLESTAT* also. This is because *I/O* activity is also a contributor to the *Statistics*. Hence these two *Tables* should be located outside the *Sys Tablespace*. As was mentioned above, since *UTLBSTAT* and *UTLESTAT* *create* and *drop* some *Tables* at each *Startup* and *Shutdown* of the database, the *Tablespace* as well as the *Tables* containing the *Statistics* get fragmented. So, these two *Tables* need to be located outside the *Sys*. But if these two *Tables* are outside the *Sys,* i.e., outside our database, a *Db_Link* to *Sys* is needed to access them. These two

*Table*s are kept in a remote database. Once *Db_Link* is *created*, login to the remote database, change the *Sys* password to some new password, go back to remote database and run the *Statistics* scripts. When the *Statistics* run is completed, reset *Sys* password. In this case the *Table*s containing *statistics* are stored in remote data *Tablespace. The Db_Block_ Statistics* so generated relate to *Library Cache, System-wide Wait Events, Average Length of Dirty Buffer Write-queue, File I/O, File I/O summed by Tablespace, Latch Statistics, No-waits Gets of Latches, RBS, Initn..Ora Values, Data_ Dictionary_Cache* etc.

Column	Description
Name	SGA component name
Bytes	Size of the memory area in bytes

Illustration 4. 1 - V$Sgastat Column Description

Some of the *Statistics* and their use in preventive measures are described here. The size of *SGA* can be obtained by querying the *Table V$Sgastat* as described in Illustration 4.1. In Illustration 4.2, an object that is frequently executed (high *Executions*) and reloaded (high *Loads*) implies that the *Shared_Pool_Size* parameter needs to be enhanced. *Pins* tells you how many *Users* kept the object in the memory.

Before starting *UTLBSTAT/UTLESTAT* (or *SQL TRACE*), set the parameter *Timed_Statistics* in the *Initn.Ora* file equal to 'TRUE'. In the most recent version of Oracle, this parameter can be set while the database is running. The call is:

```
SQL> Alter System set
     Timed_Statistics = TRUE;
```

The default value is 'FALSE'.

Excessive large values for the *Reloads* and *Invalidations* columns of the *Library Cache Statistics* in the *Report.txt* indicate Excessive *Reparsing*.

If a *User* is *created* without a default *Tablespace* assignment, then such *User*'s default *Tablespace* will be *System Tablespace* and consequently the *System Tablespace* will experience high *I/O* traffic as well as *Fragmentation*. **It may be noted that he *I/O* Statistics from *Report.txt* and *V$Filestat* are exclusively for Oracle database files.**

Column	Description
Owner	Owner of the object
Name	Name of the object
Db_Link	Database link if any
Namespace	Library Cache namespace of the object (Table/Cluster etc)
Type	Area consumed by the object in the memory
Loads	Number of times the object has been loaded
Executions	Total number of times the object has been executed
Locks	Number of Users currently locking the object
Pins	Number of Users curently pinning the object.
Kept	Yes if the object has been pinned in the Shared SQL Pool. No if it is not pinned

Illustration 4.2 - Column Description of Table V$DbObject_Cache

4.1   Library Cache

This is an important memory area and it contains *Shared SQL* and *PL/SQL* areas. From the *Statistics* collected herein, one can get an idea if the shared SQL statements are being reparsed due to insufficient memory in the cache. Its health can be gauged from the result of the following query:

```
SQL> Select Sum(Reloads)/(Sum(PINS)*100
     Libcache from V$Libcache;
```

Result: Libcache
           0.159

Excessive reparsing is reflected by large values for the *Reloads* and *Invalidations* columns of the *Library Cache Statistics* in the *Report.txt* file. Objects can be pinned in the *Library_Cache* so that they remain in the memory until they are unpinned or the *Instance* is shut down.

The result of the above query tells us that instead of ideal value of zero (i.e., no reparsing in the cache), roughly 1.6% of the statements are being reparsed. The situation may be remedied by slightly increasing the memory and checking the ratio again. In order to change the memory here, the *Initn.Ora* file is to be opened and the parameter, *Shared_Pool_Size*, has to be changed, the *Instance* to be *Shutdown* and restarted. Then the new parameter takes effect.

Library_Cache is the most tunable component of the shared *SQL pool*. It stores SQL statements and PL/SQL blocks including *Procedures, Packages and Triggers* issued in the database. These statements are already parsed and ready for execution. As in the case of *Db_Block_Buffers*, the SQL statements are managed in the *Library_Cache* by *LRU* algorithm. So all old statements are purged out of the *Library_Cache*. Each SQL statement in the *Library_Cache* has an entry in the Shared SQL area. The aim of tuning the *Library_Cache* is to avoid parsing to the minimum possible by reusing the information available in the shared SQL area of the *Library_Cache*. The application programmer has to be extremely cautious in formulating the SQL queries. Let us assume that the application programmer has posed the following query first.

```
SQL> Select * from URKRao.Tell_Det;
```

The statement is parsed and the information is kept in the shared SQL area. But in order to use this information, subsequent query by the next *User* or same application programmer **must be identical** to the earlier statement that generated the parsed information lying in the SQL area. It may be noted that the following queries do not use the above parsed information, although they appear to be identical to the above query. This results in unnecessary visit to the database for the same information.

```
SQL> Select * from URKRao.TELL_DET;

SQL> Select * from   URKRao.Tell_Det;

SQL> Select * FROM URKRao.Tell_Det;
```

Different spacings or different case of lettering in the query will make it a totally different query and hence needs physical read (disk read).

4.2   Data_Dictionary_Cache

The *Data_Dictionary* must be referenced each time a *User* issues a request for data.   The objective of providing the *Data_Dictionary_Cache* is to keep as much information about the database structures and objects in the memory as possible in order to reduce visits to the disk. This is another important memory space and its performance can be gauged from the result of the following query.

```
SQL> Select Sum(Getmisses)/Sum(Gets)*100
     Ddcache   from V$Rowcache;

Result: Ddcache
            1.9
```

This number denotes the number of misses and the value of 1.9 is satisfactory since the ideal value should be less than 10%. If for any one of the objects a value much larger than 10 is obtained, then additional memory may be provided for *Shared_Pool_Size* so that this value comes down to 10%. Some of the columns in the *Table V$Rowcache* are shown in Illustration 4.3.

Parameter	Gets	Misses
Dc_Segments		
Dc_Users		
Dc_Objects		
Dc_Tablespaces		

Illustration 4.3 - Columns of V$Rowcache

4.3   Threaded Server Session Memory

From our database we obtained the following result:

Session Memory (Bytes) Max at Session = 40,152 bytes whereas the *Shared_Pool_ Size SGA* (Bytes) = 3,500,000 bytes. Ideally, Shared_Pool_Size memory should at least be equal to or greater than the maximum session memory.

4.4   Overall Statistics

Just like there is hit ratio for the *Shared_Pool_Size*, similar *Statistics* can also collected for *Db_Block_Buffer*. The query to obtain data in this context is:

```
SQL> Select name, value from V$Sysstat where
     name IN ('Db Block Gets',
     'Consistent Gets', 'Physical Reads'):
```

`Result:`

Name	Value
Db Block Gets	142924
Consistent Gets	124556
Physical Reads	10394

Illustration 4.4 - Part of the Output of the Table V\$Sysstat

A typical output of *Db_Block_Buffer Statistics* is given in the Illustration 4.4. From these, *Hitratio* is calculated as:

Hitratio = (*Logical Reads* - *Physical Reads*) / (*Logical Reads*)

where *Logical Reads* = (*Consistent Gets* + *Db Block Gets*)

Thus *Hitratio* = {(((142924 + 124556) - 10394)/ 267480}* 100 = 96%

In another *Instance*, the *Statistics* are shown in Illustration 4.5. (*Physical Reads* mean those read from the disk rather than from the memory).

Statistics	Total	Per transaction	Per Log On
Consistent Gets	1358	1358	226.33
Db Block Gets	214	214	
Physical Reads	103	103	17.17

Illustration 4.5 - Typical Output of Statistics

This ratio tells us how well the *Db_Block_Buffer_Cache* is handling the requests for data. If all the requests are handled by *Logical Reads* without going to database files, then it is an ideal situation.

In the above set of *statistics*,

71

Overall Hitratio = {(((1358 + 214) - 103) / (1358 + 214)}*100 = 93%

A value of about 65% or higher for the *Overall Hitratio* is considered good . If the value falls below 65%, corrective action calls for increase in *Db_Block_Buffer* parameter in *Initn.Ora* file. The *Db Block Gets* value indicates the access to current copies of the data blocks. The *Consistent Gets* value indicates the access to the read-consistent copies of the blocks built from *RBS*. The total of these two provides the sum of *Logical Reads*. The *Physical Reads* are the disk reads.

The *Db_Block_Buffer* has two lists: the dirty list and the *LRU* list. The former contains the data that have been modified and awaiting *write* to disk. The latter keeps the most recently used blocks in memory.

It was mentioned earlier that whenever full *Table* retrieval takes place, the data is usually kept in the lowest priority of the *LRU* lists, ready to be purged out. This is because such requests are expected to be minimal. If full *Table* scans are to be used frequently such as in record groups, where the *Tables* are small, it is better if such *Tables* are kept in *Cache* while *creating* the *Table*.

4.5   Disk I/O Traffic

Suppose we have a departmental stores where vaious items are stored according to some pattern. Due to excessive demand for some items, a few aisles are over crowded by customers whereas others are not. There will be *contention* and the turnover will slow down due to this. Instead, suppose the most popular items in these busy aisles are distributed over different aisles which are a little more away from each other, then the crowd will be distributed evenly over several aisles. This is exactly what happens in the database disks. Database is distributed over several disks. A *Contention* occurs when a process competes with another process for the same resource simultaneously. Some files experience high *I/O* activity whereas others do not. In that case, to avoid *contention*, files with high *I/O* traffic have to be separated from each other by placing them on different disks. Before doing that, the locations of all the files are to be noted. The following query will be useful in this context.

```
SQL> Select * from Dba_Data_Files;
```

Its output is given in Illustration 4.6.

Other rows in my database are for the *Tablespaces*: *RollBack_Data/Temp_Data/System/User_Data (another)* */Org_Name.*

After a while when you monitor the statistics of I/O for different files in the disks, you come to know which files experience large traffic and which do not. In order to reduce the *contention*, the busy files may be distributed over different disks resulting in even distribution of load for all disks. For example, the I/O traffic on two files is indicated in Illustration 4.7.

The first *Datafile* has much large number of reads compared to the second file. Therefore files in this *Datafile* with 125 *Reads* should be distributed to other disks. This is similar for other such *Datafiles.*

File_Name	File_Id
C:\Orant\database\USR10RCL.Ora	2

Ts_ Name	Bytes	Blocks	Status	Rel FNo	Auto Ext
User_ Data	3,145,728	1536	Available	2	Yes

Max Bytes	Max Blocks	Incr_By
1,57,286,400	76,800	2560

Illustration 4.6 - Typical Dba_Data_Files Output

Datafile	Reads
C:\ORAWIN\DBS\MMS.ORA	125
C:\ORAWIN\DBS\MNS.SYS	11

Illustration 4.7 - Reads of Different Datafiles

4.6   Latch Statistics

By using SQL query one can obtain information about *No_Wait* entries. *No_Wait Hitratio* is defined as:

No_Wait Hitratio = No_Wait_Gets/(No_Wait_Gets +

No_Wait_Misses)

The *Gets* are understood to be 100% if the *Hitratio* comes out as 1. This the ideal situation. That means there is no waiting due to latches. If the ratio is < 1 then the number of latches should be increased.

4.7   RBS Contention

When a transaction commences, an entry into Rollback segments (*RBS*) will be made. Although several *RBSs* exist, the entry has to be within one *RBS*. It can not overflow into the next *RBS*. Neither can the whole entry be transferred into another larger *RBS*. That means, every transaction should fit into one *RBS*. If the *RBSs* provided are inadequate, then *contention* takes place. If the *Satistics* collection on an *RBS* is started, this *contention* is computed and entered into the *Report.txt*. Ideally the observed *contention* counts should be less than 1% of the total gets. If the *contention* is more, the remedy is to create more *RBS*.

4.8   Redolog Buffer Contention

The *Redolog* buffer should be adequately sized to reduce waiting period for events. The *Redolog* buffer of the *SGA* stores all changes made to the database. They include *Insert, Delete and Update* statements and all *DDL* statements. The *V$System_Event View* contains information on the *System-wide Waits* for an event as given in Illustration 4.8.

Column	Description
Event	Name of the event waited for
Total_Waits	Total No of timeouts for the event
Time_Waited	Total amount of time waited for the event in 10 msec units
Average_Wait	Average amount of time waited for the event in 10 msec units

Illustration 4.8 - Description of V$System_Event Table Columns

If the number of *Total_Waits* is large, then the *Log_Buffer* parameter should be increased. The transactions that are waiting to be written to *Redolog* files from the *Redolog* buffer allow us to recover the database in case of an unexpected crash of the *Instance*. In other words, If the *Redolog* buffers fill up and *LGWR* does not write the *Redolog* buffers to *Redolog* files, then Oracle stops. Since the *Redolog* buffers are not overwritten, there is a waiting period till the existing data is first written to the *Redolog* files. This is *Redolog* buffer *contention*. This *contention* ideally should be zero. If not, the remedy is to increase the *Log_Buffer* parameter in *Initn.Ora* file.

4.9   Sort Memory Contention

The following type of queries result in sorting of the data.

Select distinct/Select unique/Select.. group by/Create index

Oftentimes, the data from the disk are to be brought over to the memory area to be processed only after sorting. For example, we may bring the salary data of employees and then sort them according to the designation. To facilitate that, *Sort Memory Area* is provided. This sort area is limited. Since memory areas are faster than disk, sorting is done fast in this *Sort* area. However, if the data to be sorted is very large, sorting is done on the disk itself. If insufficient *Sort Memory Area* is provided, then *contention* takes place and it takes much longer to sort the data. One can measure *Sorts*(Memory) and *Sorts*(Disk) *contention*. If either of them is large, then appropriate additional memory or disk space is to be provided. For enhancing the memory, the *Sort_Area_Size* parameter in the *Initn.Ora* file should be enhanced.

The query to obtain this *contention* is:

```
SQL> Select name, value from V$Sysstat
     where name like '%sort%';
```

The result is tabulated in Illustration 4.9

Name	Value
Sorts(Memory)	234126
Sorts(Disk)	30
Sorts(Rows)	75234036

Illustration 4.9 -Typical Output from V$Sysstat

Contention = {*Sorts*(Disk)/*Sorts*(Memory)}$* 100 = 0.013\%$

which is acceptable.

All disk sorts are performed in *User*'s assigned *Temporary Tablespace*. If not assigned, *System Tablespace* will be used for the *User* as the *Temporary Tablespace* for sorting.

4.10   Problematic SQL Statements

SQL Trace is used to generate *Statistics* into a trace file which is formatted using *Tkprof.sql*. The *SQL Trace* can be used to identify the SQL statements that consume the most resources and that are executed more often.

The *Hitratio* of *Shared_SQL_Pool* (*Library_Cache* + *Data_Dictionary_Cache*) tells you how often the information requested by a process was already located in the shared pool without requiring *Physical Reads* from the disk. The default size of the *Shared_SQL_Pool* is 3.5 x 10 E6 bytes.

A private SQL area has *Persistent* and *Run Time Areas*. The *Persistent Area* uses memory in the *Library_Cache* for open cursors.

Dbms_Shared_Pool package is used by Oracle for PL/SQL objects to be *pinned (kept)* in the shared *SQL Pool Area*. Once *pinned*, the object remains there until explicitly *unpinned* or database is *shutdown*.

The commands for *pinning* and *unpinning* are:

```
SQL> Execute
     Dbms_Shared_Pool.keep(URKRAO.Account);
SQL> Execute
     Dbms_Shared_Pool.unkeep(URKRAO.Account);
```

These are a few of the many ways in which the health of the database can be monitored and remedial measures applied when necessary. This gives only a flavour of what Oracle can do to enhance its own performance.

Chapter 5   Security in Oracle

It is obvious that access to database and its objects should be jealously guarded so that unauthorised persons or novices may not access/tamper with it. For example, Enquiry desk clerks in the Bank may have access just to "*Select*" *Privilege* on a particular *Table* containing information of the various accounts of the customers to answer their queries. The desk clerks should not have "*Delete*" or "*Update*" *Privileges* to any *Table*. Otherwise they may inadvertently or willfully tamper with the accounts of customers. Similarly in an organisation, HRD staff may not be allowed to access the work reports of the employees. The Leave account clerk need not have access to the *Table* containing details of salary of employees. Oracle has provisions to precisely control access to different *Users* to different degrees. Even at column level of a *Table*, access can be controlled. The beauty with Oracle is that this access can be *granted* to anybody and can be *revoked (withdrawn)* at will, if necessity arises. Thus high level security is provided for Oracle database.

First and foremost, to access the database, one has to access the server on which the database runs, i.e., its platform. After that, the *Operating System* should be shielded from the *User*s since they are not concerned with many files, such as *Redolog* files therein.

5.1   User Account

*User*s of the database have to be *created* and identified properly. Hence a *User* account is first created as follows:

```
SQL> Create User Ganpat identified
     by mooshika default Tablespace Org_Name
     temporary Tablespace Temp;
```

This way *User* by name "Ganpat" was created and the *User* is identified by a password "mooshika". The password can be changed at will by the *User*. The default *Tablespace* in the *Org_Name Tablespace* implies that unlimited space is allotted to the *User*. The *User* can use *Temp Tablespace* for all temporary transactions, such as sorting data. Since there is no specific allotment of space for the *User* in the above SQL command, the *User* can not create any object in the database. Further, there is no profile for the *User* in the command, and hence the *User* can use, what is called a default profile endowed with unlimited resources. The *User* is then given a quota in the *Tablespace* by the following command:

```
SQL> Alter Ganpat
     quota 50M on Org_Name;
```

This allots a space of 50 MB on the *Org_Name Tablespace* for "Ganpat". If *Temp Tablespace* is not assigned to a *User*, the *User* automatically gets *System Tablespace* as temporary *Tablespace*. The password can be changed by the following command.

```
SQL> Alter User Ganpat identified by
     agajanana;
```

Here "agajanana" is the new password in place of old "mooshika". *Sys* owns *Data_Dictionary* and is the *User* to which one connects when one connects *Internal*. *Sys* has a *DBA Role*. *System* also manages the database and has a *DBA Role*. One cannot drop a *User_Id* that owns objects in an Oracle database. Objects can be transfered to another *User* as follows:

```
SQL> Create Table RAM.Greetings as
     Select * from SAM.Greetings;
```

Similarly transfer all other objects of "SAM" to "RAM". Now "SAM" can be dropped.

Sometimes it happens that one *User,* having lots of *Tables* in his account, has left the organisation and one would like to drop the *User* along with his objects. The call is:

```
SQL> Drop User SAM cascade;
```

There is no *Rollback* **for this command.** Therefore one has to be very careful with this command. If "SAM's" account needs to be temporarily disabled, the command is:

```
SQL> Revoke Create Session to SAM;
```

In order to access a database by connecting to that database, the *User* should have "**Create Session**" privilege.

Sometimes one is interested in knowing who all are logged in at a given time. The command for this is:

```
SQL> Select SID, SerialNo, Status, User_Name
     from V$Session;
```

The output will be similar to that given in Illustration 5.1.

SID	SerialNo	Status	User_Name
1	222	Active	DBSNMP
2	333	Active	SYS
3	444	Inactive	STD002

Illustration 5.1 - User Status

This information will help in selectively killing a session. The following command can be used for this purpose.

```
SQL> Alter System kill session 'SID,
     SerialNo';
```

In Oracle 7, there is a provision for nearly 40 object level *Privileges* and equal number of database management *Privileges* that can be *granted* to *User*s. For example, the object level *Privileges* include *Create Index, Create Trigger, Create Synonym, Create View, Select any Table, Update any Table* etc. These can also be assigned along with the *Table* name so that the *Privilege* is confined to that (not any other) *Table*. Similarly some chosen *User*s may be given special *Privileges* called database management *Privileges* to enable them to perform *DBA* duties. These include *Create Role, Alter Tablespace, Alter User, Drop User, Audit Database, Grant any Privilege, Grant any Role, Drop Profile* etc. **It may be added here that no *Privileges* are grantable on *Indexes and Triggers*.**

5.2 Roles

Oracle 7 introduced *Roles* and it is very versatile. This is like a designation. An employee in an organisation can be given a designation such as Clerk, Assistant_Manager, Manager etc. Each designation endows the person with some powers to perform specific duties. For example, a Manager assigns duty posts to different employees, he also pays their wages, draws money or deposits money into the company's bank accounts. Similarly, a Clerk is allowed to make entries of sales/purchases in the books of accounts. A Cashier deals with paying cash and debiting to accounts, and receiving cash and crediting to accounts, but does not have access to any other information of the database. So once you assign an employee a designation such as Manager or Cashier or Clerk, the type of access to the database is fixed, and all employees with that designation will have identical access *Privileges* to the database. This designation is known as *Role*. In Oracle a *Role* is *created* with predetermined access *Privileges* depending upon the duties to be performed. The *Role* can be assigned to any number of employees with identical duties. This way you avoid *granting* each privilege to each employee individually.

81

5.2.1 Role Creation

In order to use the *Role*, the developer should have an idea of what the job of the *Role* is and therefrom what *Privileges* are to be *granted* to this *Role*. Then the *Role* is assigned to *User*s who inherit all the *Privileges* assigned to the *Role*. The steps involved are:

- *Creation* of *Role* "Manager"

  ```
  SQL> Create Role Manager;
  ```

- *Granting Privileges* to the *Role*

  ```
  SQL> Grant procedure, Create Table,
       Delete Table to Manager;
  ```

- *Create* an User

  ```
  SQL> Create User Ganpat identified
       by mooshika;
  ```

- Assign Manager *Role* to *User* "Ganpat".

  ```
  SQL> Grant Manager to Ganpat;
  ```

In the creation of *Role*, a password can be assigned as matter of abundant caution.

```
SQL> Create Role Manager identified by Boss;
```

Oracle 6 has three *System* level *Privilege Roles,* namely, *Connect, Resource and DBA*. In order to facilitate upgradation of Oracle 6 to Oracle 7, the latter has retained these three *System* level versions. These *Roles* have several *Privileges*. *DBA Role* has an additional facility called *Admin* option.

Oracle 7 provided a new *Role OSOPER* expressly to enable some *Users* to be assigned this *Role* for *DBA* support. This *Role* has some of the *DBA Privileges* such as *Startup/Shutdown/Alter Database/Backup etc.*

5.3   Admin

While *granting Privileges*, there is an additional option known as *Admin* option. **A grant can be qualified with the added comment with or without *Admin* option.** If the *grant* is **with** *Admin* option, the *grantee* in turn can *grant* the *Privilege* to other *Users*. If not, the *grantee* can not *grant* the *Privilege* to other *Users*. As was mentioned earlier, *DBA* has all *System Privileges* with *Admin* option.

5.4   Profile

It was mentioned earlier that a default *Profile* exists in Oracle 7 with many unlimited facilities such as size of the *Tablespace*. These facilities can be controlled by specifying the *Profile*. For example, resources like the *Connect_Time* for the database can be specified for the *Profile*.

System Privileges give a little more access to the database. For example, it allows you to *grant Privileges* assigned to your account to others. But before obtaining the *System Privileges*, you should already have some other *Privileges*. For example, unless you have *Create Table* privilege, you can not get the *Snapshot Privilege*.

***Delete* is a very restrictive *Privilege* and it allows a *User* to delete rows but it does not allow the *User* to drop the *Table*.** *Truncate* rather than *Delete* should be used to remove data from a *Table* since this does not cost any *RBS* space. ***Truncate* implies *Commit*.**

You can appreciate how fine tuning exists in the security of data in Oracle. The *Update Privilege* allows *User* to change the contents of an existing row of the data. **It does not allow new rows to be created** or existing ones to be *deleted*.

5.5 Grant

If you *created* database objects such as *Tables, Indexes* and *Sequences,* you are supposed to "own" these objects and hence you can assign *Privileges* on these objects to other *Users*. But the overriding authority, *DBA*, can also assign the *Privileges* on any object of the database including on those you own, to any *User*. The following SQL commands do the job.

- **Table Creation**

    ```
    SQL> Grant Create Table to URKRao;
        (To User "URKRao")

    SQL> Grant Create Table to Manager;
        (To A Role "Manager")

    SQL> Grant Create Table to URKRao,
            Reddy;
        (To multiple "Users")
    ```

- **Select**

    ```
    SQL> Grant Select on URKRao.Tell_Det
            to Reddy;
    ```

    By this command, the *DBA* (Or any *User* with *DBA Role*) can *grant Select Privilege* to *User* "Reddy" on the *Table Tell_Det created* (and owned) by *User* "URKRao".

- *Granting Privileges*

  ```
  SQL> Grant Select on Tell_Det to
       Ganpat with Admin option;
  ```

  This allows *User* "Ganpat" to *grant Select* on
  Tell_Det to other *Users*.

- **Altering Privileges**

  No *User* can be allowed to have the *Privilege* to
  consume all the space in every *Tablespace*. In order to
  control and limit the space, the following command
  grants the space.

  ```
  SQL> Alter User Ganpat quota 20MB on
       User_Data;
  ```

  This allows *User* Ganpat to utilise 20 MB space in the
  Tablespace named *User_Data*.

  Instead of *granting* the *Privileges* one by one, you
  may club all scripts of the *grants* together in one
  grant.sql file ending in a back slash. That file can be
  run with @*grants.sql* command to *grant* all *Privileges*
  to all employees in one go.

- **Drop**

  As was mentioned earlier, the authority which *creates*
  these *Roles* is also the authority which *drops* these
  Roles. The command for *dropping* a *Role* is:

  ```
  SQL> Drop Role Manager;
  ```

- **Revoke**

  It makes sense that the authority which *grants* these *Privileges/Roles* should also be the authority to withdraw these *Grants/Roles*. It is the case with Oracle. The following command does the job.

  ```
  SQL> Revoke Create Table from
       URKRao;
  ```

5.6   Some Views of Privileges

There are several views involving the *Privileges* provided by Oracle. Some are given below.

5.6.1   Dba_Sys_Privs

This query is used to know the *Sys* privileges *grantable* to *Users*.

```
SQL> Select * from Dba_Sys_Privs;
```

In our database this query returned 200 rows. Some of these rows are given in Illustration 5.2.

Grantee	Privilege	Admin_Option
Sys	Delete any Table	No
Sys	Execute any type	No
Sys	Select any sequence	No
Mohan	Unlimited Tablespace	No
Connect	Alter Session	No
Connect	Create View	No
DBA	Alter Session	Yes

Illustration 5.2 - Output of Dba_Sys_Privs

5.6.2   Dba_Role_Privs

This query shows the *Roles* that are *granted* to the *Users*.

```
SQL> Select * from Dba_Role_Privs;
```

This returned 190 rows in our database. Three of the rows are shown in Illustration 5.3.

Grantee	Granted_Role	Admin_Option	Default_Role
URKRao	Clerk	Yes	Yes
URKRao	Connect	No	Yes
URKRao	Resource	No	Yes

Illustration 5.3 - Typical Output of Dba_Role_Privs

5.6.3   Dba_Tab_Privs

This tells us about the *Table Privileges granted* by the owner on his *Tables* to other *User*.

```
SQL> Select * from Dba_Tab_Privs;
```

This query with owner = "URKRao" returned 24 rows for the following 6 columns. One of these rows is shown in Illustration 5.4.

Granter	Owner	Table _Name	Grantee	Privi- lege	Admin
URKRao	URKRao	Tell _Hd	Ganpat	Select	Yes

Illustration 5.4 - Typical Output of Dba_Tab_Privs

Chapter 6   Rollback Segments

The *Rollback Segment* (*RBS*) is a sort of an addendum to the *Db_Block_Buffer*. All the data from SQL queries are brought over into the *Db_Block_Buffer*. However, if the data is undergoing any process, such as an *Update,* and going to stay for some time without *Commit* or *Rollback,* then the data will be shifted to *RBS*. This is especially true if space is needed for new data in the *Db_Block_Buffer*. *Locks* are held for the duration of the transaction to prevent destructive interaction from other processes or transactions. A *Commit or Rollback* releases the *lock.*

The *RBSs* are one of most expensive memory areas in Oracle. This is because of the nature of their performance. They contain the "before" image of the data undergoing a transaction like *Update.*

To start with, *RBS* captures the "before image" of the data that existed prior to a transaction of a *User.* At this stage, queries from other *Users* against this data that is being changed, will return the data as it existed before the change. After the transactions, if the *User* issues a command,

```
SQL> Rollback;
```

then transactions that are made on the data get undone. This *Rollback* command is available for three transactions: *Update/Insert/Delete.* So one can appreciate the importance of *RBS*. For an *RBS*, *Pctinc* should always be kept = 0. The amount of *RBS* activity generated by the statements go in the order: *Insert<<Delete<<Update.*

As was mentioned earlier, a database will have multiple *RBSs*. The first *RBS* to be *created* in the database is in the *System Tablespace*. When the database is *created,* the *System RBS* automatically gets *created.* This *System RBS* is used to manage database level transactions such as *Data Dictionary Table* modifications etc. In addition, a second *RBS* is also *created* in the database in the *System Tablespace* for future use and hence is kept inactive. The way the two *System RBSs* are *created* is as follows:

- By using the *Create Database* command, implicitly the first *System RBS* gets created.

- *Create* a second *RBS* in the *System Tablespace.*

- Make the second *RBS* available.

- *Create* other *Tablespaces.*

- *Create* a new *Tablespace* titled *RBS* (to accommodate 5 *RBS*s).

- *Create* five *RBS*s in the *RBS Tablespace.*

- Deactivate the second *RBS* in *System Tablespace.*

- Activate 4 out of 5 *RBS*s in the *RBS Tablespace.*

In order to find out the size, location and other information related to the *RBS*s in a database, the following command may be issued.

```
SQL> Select * from Dba_Segments
     where Segment_Type = 'Rollback';
```

This *Table* has 19 columns. In our database the output had 20 rows. One of them is given in Illustration 6.1.

Other rows in the *Table* below pertain to Segment_Names: *Sys.system, Sys.Rb_Temp, Sys.Rb1 to Sys.Rb16* (Total 18). A given *RBS* can be private and belong only to that particular *Instance.* If it is Public, it is available to all *Users.* It will be seen later that, if needed, a particular *RBS* can be reserved exclusively for a particular transaction for some specific purpose (Section 6.5)

89

and once the purpose is served, the *RBS* can be released for public use.

Ow-ner	Seg_ Name	Part_ Name	Seg_ Type	Ts_ Name	Header File	Header Block
SYS	Sysrol 1		RBS	Org_ Name	6	9517

Bytes	Blocks	Extents	Init_ Ext	Next_ Ext
20,971,520	10,240	2	10,485,760	10,485,760

Min_ Ext	Max_ Ext	Pctinc	Free Lists	Free ListGP	RelF No	Buffer Pool
2	121	0	1	1	6	Default

Illustration 6.1 - Typical Output from Dba_Segments for RBS

Let us see how the *RBS*s handle multiple entries. If there are 5 *RBS*s, the database allows entries into each *RBS* in a round robin fashion as shown in Illustration 6.2.

The first entry E1 goes to *RBS* #1. The next entry E2 goes to *RBS* #2 and so on up to *RBS* #4. Every set of *RBS*s should have *Freespace* set apart for future use which is inactive and it cannot be used. In our set of *RBS*s, *RBS* # 5 is set apart for *Freespace*. The next entry E5 is assigned to *RBS* #1 and so on and so forth.

One may wonder why five *RBS*s are there instead of one large *RBS* of capacity equivalent to all the five put together. The reason is simple. Many concurrent transactions might vie with each other to get into the *RBS* at the same time. Then there will be *contention*. Five different ones will mitigate that problem. In that case why not have many still smaller sized *RBS*s. This is not acceptable in view of our earlier observation that any such entry should fit into one *Extent* or at the most into one full *RBS*. If it occupies more than one *Extent*, then *wrapping* takes place. Besides, it can not overflow into the next *RBS*. That means a transaction can not span more than one *RBS*. Even a moderately small transaction may not fit into a *RBS*, if it is too small.

RBS # 1	E1	E5	

RBS # 2	E2	

RBS # 3	E3	

RBS # 4	E4	

RBS # 5	

Illustration 6.2 - Filling Up of RBS

The *RBS* may be manipulated through SQL command as follows:

6.1   RBS Creation

```
SQL> Create public Rollback Segment RB01
     Tablespace RBS;
```

This will *create* a Public *RBS* named *Rb01* with default storage parameters in the *Tablespace RBS*. The default parameters are: *Initial* 125K, *Next* 125K, *Minext* 18, *Maxext* 999.

The parameters of an *RBS* can not be changed. It has to be dropped first and recreated with changed parameters. In order to drop the *RBS*, it has to be offline first. The following is the sequence of commands to change the parameters of an existing   *RBS*, designated *RB01*.

```
SQL> Alter Rollback Segment RB01 OFFLINE;
```

This will make the *RB01 Offline.*

```
SQL> Drop Rollback Segment RB01;
```

This will drop the *RB01.*

```
SQL> Create Public Rollback Segment RB01
     Tablespace RBS
     storage (initial 1M
     next 1M
     pctincrease 0
     optimal 2M
     minext 2
     maxext 100)

SQL> Alter Rollback Segment RB01 ONLINE;
```

This will bring the *RB01* into *Online.* **For obvious reasons the *System RBS* cannot be dropped by the above set of commands**.

In order to know the number of *RBSs* available, look at the *Rollback Segment* parameter in the *Initn.Ora. Rollback Segments* = (r0, r1, r2, r3) denotes that four *RBSs*, r0 to r3 are available.

It was mentioned earlier that a given *RBS* can be reserved for a particular transaction.   A situation may arise wherein the transaction is large and requires a full *RBS* exclusively for that transaction (Section 7.5). In such a case, an *RBS* can be set apart for that purpose.

6.2   Rollback Entries

As Oracle tries to write a *RBS* entry of a transaction that had just begun, there is a restriction that the entry should ideally fit into one *Extent* in the *RBS* otherwise *wrapping* into neighbouring

92

Extents takes place. At the same time, as the entry gets larger than the *Extents* available in that *RBS*, the entry en masse can not be transferred into another larger empty *RBS*. What happens then? Let us see with some illustration of an *RBS* with total 6 *Extents*, Ext1 empty, Ext2 in use and four more *Extents* (Ext3 to Ext6) empty.

Ext1	Ext2	Ext3	Ext4	Ext5	Ext6
Empty	In Use	Trans2	Trans2	Trans2	Trans2

Illustration 6.3 - RBS Entries

In Illustration 6.3, the transaction Trans2 is being written into the *Extent* Ext3 of the *RBS* and goes up to the Ext6, the last *Extent* in that *RBS*. If the entry needs one more *Extent*, it cannot spill over into another *RBS*. It will look for empty *Extents* in the same *RBS*. Ext1 will be considered and it is currently free. When the transaction is entered fully, it would have occupied *Extents* 3, 4, 5, 6 and 1. What if the *Extent* 1 was not free? Where can it find the required one *Extent* space in that *RBS*? Oracle provides for remedying such situations. The *RBS*, which is full, dynamically acquires an additional *Extent* Ext7 by the side of Ext6 (i.e., contiguous with Ext6) and will complete the transaction. This additional space comes from the *Freespace* (Section 6.2 *RBS* #5) provided in the set of *RBS*s. The unfortunate part of this is that, even after the transaction that forced the *RBS* to acquire the additional *Extent* is completed, the *RBS's* additional space of Ext7 is retained. Thus if several large transactions are performed during busy periods of the database operation, these transactions rob additional *Extents* from the *Freespace* from *RBS* #5 and will wipe out all the *Freespace* available. Thus other *RBS*s cannot acquire such *Extents* if need arises. Fortunately, Oracle takes care of such abnormalities. By assigning a parameter, *Optimal*, in the *Initn.Ora* file, if the *RBS* expands beyond the size denoted by *Optimal*, the *RBS* at the conclusion of the transaction dynamically shreds its excess size by shrinking back to the *Optimal* size.

6.3   Details of RBS

At some stage, one would like to know the details such as the numbers, names, availability, size, status etc. of the *RBS*s in the database. There are two SQL commands to get this information. One is:

```
SQL> Select * from Dba_Rollback_Segs;
```

In my database, the following output is obtained as shown in Illustration 6.4 (one of many rows is shown). The value for InstanceNo in the illustration as NULL indicates that the *RBS* belongs to a single *Instance*. Further, *Status* can have several values with different meanings as indicated in Illustration 6.5.

Segment_ Name	Owner	Ts_Name	Segment_Id	File_Id
Sysroll	Public	Org_Name	18	6

Block_Id	Init_Ext	Next_Ext	Min_Ext	Max_Ext
9517	10485760	10485760	2	121

Pctinc	Status	InstanceNo	RelFNo
0	Offline		6

Illustration 6.4 - Typical Output of Dba_RollBack_Segs

Status		Value
In Use	means	RBS is Online
Available	means	RBS was created but it is not Online
Offline	means	RBS is Offline
Invalid	means	RBS was dropped
Needs Recovery	means	RBS has some data that cannot be rolledback

Illustration 6.5 - Different Possible Values for Status of an RBS

The output from the following query is given in Illustration 6.1.

```
SQL>   Select * from Dba_Segments
       where Segment_Type = 'ROLLBACK';
```

This will show 19 columns. Among these columns, the *Header_File* is the file in which first *Extent* of the *RBS* is stored. In this *Table*, the parameter *Optimal* does not appear. If one wants to learn about the *Optimal* size parameter of the *RBS*, one has to query what are known as the dynamic performance *Tables, V$Rollstat and V$Rollname*. The columns of the *Table V$Rollstat* are shown in Illustration 6.6.

```
SQL> Select N.name, S.OPTSIZE
     from V$Rollstat S, V$Rollname N
     where N.USN = S.USN;
```

This query will give the name of the *RBS* and its *Optimal* parameter. We have seen earlier that in order to design a database working at its optimum efficiency, you have to tell the *DBA* many of your requirements and what you want to do with the database. In addition to your requirement of *Tablespace*, you also have to tell him the nature of interaction of your application with the database. The latter part of your requirement decides the size and number of *RBS*s the *DBA* has to provide for your requirement. The *DBA* collects such information from all the *User*s and then determines the overall requirements for *Tables, RBS*s etc. We shall see how you can assess your requirement of *RBS*.

6.4   Estimation of RBS Size

In order to assess the requirement of *RBS* for our application, we have to determine the number and type of transactions that use the *RBS*. That means we have to determine first what is the total amount of *RBS* entry data that remains at any given time in the *RBS* without either *committing* or *rolling back*. This is known as

Active entry. There is also another type of entry in the *RBS* known as *Inactive_In_Use* entry. These are the *committed* or *rolledback* entries that did not leave the *RBS* since the data was being used by other processes such as long running queries. For *Inactive_In_Use* entries, *RBS* acts like an extended *Db_Block_Buffer*. The first type of entry is sufficient for the time being sinc,e at the same time, the second one can be avoided by postponing the long queries to a less busy time slot such as that in the night (silent hours or on a holiday).

Column	Description
USN	Rollback_Segment number
Extents	No of Extents in the RBS
RSSize	RBS size (bytes)
Writes	The no of bytes written into the RBS
Xacts	No of active entries in the RBS
Gets	No of RBS header requests
Waits	No of RBS header requests that required waits
Optsize	Optimal parameter of the RBS
HWMSize	Highest value of RBS size reached
Shrinks	No of shrinks that the RBS underwent
Wraps	No of Wraps of RBS
Extends	No of times RBS acquired additional Extents
Aveshrink	Average no of bytes released during shrinks
Aveactive	Average size of active Extents
Status	Status of the RBS

Illustration 6.6 - Description of Columns of the Table V\$Rollstat

So let us use the *Active* entries for the time being. Knowing the total volume of transactions, we can have a break-up of typical concurrent transactions of each type and their volumes. For each type, the largest and average transactions can be estimated. A typical breakup is shown in Illustration 6.7.

It may be noted that if multiple records are being *updated* in a single transaction, it is counted as one transaction. The number of *Extents* that should constitute one *RBS* capable of handling all the transactions is to be determined. In Illustration 6.7, the largest single transaction is 700 KB. This entry should fit into one *RBS* (because no entry should spill over into a second *RBS*). The thumb rule for the overheads for this are: 5% for *Header*, 20% for *Freespace*, 15% for *Inactive* data.

Type of Trans	Number of Trans	Tot Entry Volume	Avg Entry Volume	Maximum Volume
A	3	210 KB	70 KB	70 KB
B	1	500 KB	500 K	500 KB
C	20	800 KB	40 KB	40 KB
D	1	700 KB	700 KB	700 KB
E	10	500 K	50 KB	50 KB
Total	35	2710 KB		

Illustration 6.7 - Different Types of Transactions on Database

Minimum Possible Size (MPS) = (Largest transaction * 100/(100 - (*Header* + *Freespace* + *Inactive* data)) = (Largest transaction) * 100/(100 - (5 + 20 + 15))
= (700) * 100/60 = 1166 KB.

The total minimum space (space for one *RBS*) required at any one time is 1166 KB/*RBS*. Since the total entry size = 2710 KB, after providing for the above mentioned overheads of 40%, the minimum total size = sum (total entry size) * 100/60 = 2710 * 100/60 = 4516 KB. Therefore the minimum number of *RBS* units required = 4516/1166 = 4.

This needs refinement. There are two groups of transactions. In the range 40-70 KB, there are 33 transactions. In addition, there is one with 500 KB and another with 700 KB, making a total 35 concurrent transactions. Thus ideally the minimum number of *RBS* required can be 35, one for each concurrent transaction. Since this is a large number and 4 (above) is a small number, the actual compromise requirement will be somewhere in between the two

97

limits. Since the two groups of transactions (40-70 KB and 500-700 KB) differ very much in size, optimisation of *RBS* size is not easy.

Oracle suggests six transactions per *RBS* as optimum. In that case, 35 total transactions require 6 *RBS*s. Now one has to estimate the actual total size of each of these *RBS*s as well as the number of *Extents* into which each *RBS* is to be divided.

Let us make some guesses. Take 70 KB (largest size of the 33 small transactions) as the *Extent* size. Since there are 33 small-sized transactions, they need 33 * 70 = 2310 KB. If the 700 KB transaction is to be fitted into these *Extents*, 9 *Wraps* are needed. (First *Extent* 70 KB + 9 * 70 KB = 700 KB). For accommodating the 500 KB transaction, 7 *Wraps* (first *Extent* of 70 KB + 7 * 70 KB = 560 KB) are needed. For different *Extent* sizes, number of *Wraps* and space required are computed as shown in the Illustration 6.8.

Extent Size	Trans Entry	Num of Entries	Space Reqd (KB)	No of Wraps
70 KB	< 70 KB	33	2310	0
	500 KB	1	500	7
	700 KB	1	700	9
Total		35	3510	16
125 KB	< 70 KB	33	4125	0
	500 KB	1	500	3
	700 KB	1	750	5
Total		35	5375	8

Illustration 6.8 - Number of Wraps for Entries in RBS

As we increase the *Extent* size further, although number of *Wraps* decrease, the space required increases much more. As a compromise, one can choose 125 KB *Extent* size, in which case, including the overheads, the space required for transactions alone is 5375 KB * 100/60 = 9000 KB. Let us say, we chose 6 *RBS*s each with 9000/6 KB = 1500 KB per *RBS*. Thus for an *Extent* size of 125 KB, the number of *Extents* is 1500/125 = 12 for transaction entry use only. This includes all the 35 transactions since only 5375KB are considered. In addition, the *RBS Header* needs 1 *Extent*, *Inactive_In_Use* requires about 2 *Extents* and *Freespace* requires 3 *Extents* making a total of 18 *Extents* per *RBS*.

The final size of an *RBS* is 18* 125 = 2250 KB. Once you arrive at the *RBS* requirements, the rest is simple. You *create* and activate the *RBS* as follows:

6.4.1   RBS Tablespace Creation

```
SQL> Alter Tablespace   RBS;
     default storage
     (Initial 125K
     Next 125K
     Minext 18
     Maxext 999)
```

6.4.2   RBS with Optimal

```
SQL> Create RollBack Segment r1
     Tablespace RBS
     storage(optimal 2250K)
     Alter RollBack Segment r1 ONLINE;
```

As was mentioned earlier, the parameters of the *RBS* can not be changed. It has to be dropped and recreated (Section 6.1).

6.5   Entry Size in RBS

In Illustration 6.7, we assumed the sizes and numbers of transactions in an *RBS*. How did we get this? Before doing this, first we have to choose and set apart a particular *RBS* for this investigation. This can be done by the following SQL command.

```
SQL> Set transaction use
     Rollback_Segment r1;
```

This means that, henceforth, whatever transaction we are going to
perform will be directed to only the *RBS* r1. We have to determine
the *writes* to this *RBS* before performing the transaction, using the
following query.

```
SQL> Select N.Name, S.Writes
     from V$Rollname N, V$Rollstat S
     where N.USN = S.USN
```

This gives the *writes* to the *RBS* before the particular transaction,
for which we need to know the volume. After the transaction
query is performed, determine again the *writes* via the same SQL
command. The difference between the two *writes* gives the size of
the particular transaction.

6.6   UTLBSTAT AND UTLESTAT

As was mentioned earlier in the introductory remarks of Chapter
4, these utilities can be run to collect *Statistics*. From this,
information about the dynamic extension of *RBS*, number of bytes
written to *RBS*, *waits* in writing to *RBS*, size of *RBS*, number of
active transactions, number of *shrinks* that the *RBS* had to perform
to stay within the *Optimal* size and the number of times an *RBS*
entry *wrapped* from one *Extent* to another can also be obtained.

6.7   Data vs RBS

An On Line Transaction Processing (*OLTP*) *System* has high-
activity, characterised by frequent *Insert* and *Update* transactions.
This can occur in Banking or Credit card business deals. The main
criteria for this type of data is availability, speed, concurrency and
recoverability. Since it has frequently changing data, the retrieval
must be efficient. This is possible if there is good *indexing*. This

implies that the queries call for *indexing* retrieval rather than full *Table* scans. The *indexing* should not be too excessive since it may affect the *inserting*, *updating* and *deleting* processes. The transactions in here are likely to be short and hence need a *RBS* of relatively smaller size.

A Decision Support *System* (*DSS*) holds large volumes of data (such as Credit card Systems or Accounts of large companies) and is normally used for reporting purposes. Here, in contrast to *OLTP*, the queries are much larger and hence require full *Table* scans. Therefore, *indexing* is not helpful. Here one needs large *RBS* with *Extents* larger than that in the *OLTP* situation.

If one needs the same database in both *OLTP* and *DSS* types of use at different times, the former can be operated with *Indexes* whereas the latter can be operated with the *Indexes* disabled.

Chapter 7   Backup And Recovery

We have seen that redundancy is built into Oracle to take care of accidental loss of important Oracle files such as *Redolog, Control* etc. What about the redundancy for the valuable data in the database? Oftentimes, we intend to give one command and by oversight give another. In such cases there is a finite chance that we may accidentally wipe out our valuable data. Unintentionally, any *User* can drop a *Table* with data. The data may be corrupted by internal mistakes in the application. On other occasions, there may be a crash of the database and we may lose valuable data. In order to take care of such unexpected events, there are built-in checks in Oracle to enable us to recover the data. The technique to do this is known as *Backup*.

7.1   OS Backup

In the *Operating System Backup*, as the name suggests, utilities are provided by the OS to duplicate all important Oracle data files on a tape or disk drive. If the database is large, it may take long time to copy the entire database. As the copying process is going on, if *Users* are allowed to use the database, there is a minor complication. The *Users* might be *deleting, updating* and *inserting* data. Since *Backup* and *User* interaction are going on simultaneously, one can never know whether a particular file has undergone changes due to *User* interaction before or after *Backup*. This discrepancy introduces what is called lack of *consistency* of the *Backup* files.

7.2   Cold Backup

In order to get around this consistency problem, *Cold Backup* is resorted to. In this, the database is first *shutdown* and then it is *backed up*. In this *Backup*, the *Datafiles* (one *Tablespace* as a whole at a time) are copied to the tape one at a time using the *OS Copy* or *Tape Transfer* utility. The particular *Datafile* is copied in toto. All the *Tables* in a given *Datafile* are simultaneously copied in one go. So even if one *Table*, out of several in the *Datafile*, is lost during the transfer, *Backup* of the entire *Datafile* is to be repeated. In *Cold Backup*, all the *Datafiles*, the *Control* file, all *Online Redolog* files and *Initn.Ora*, defining the *Instance*, are also *backed up*, This type of *Backup* is satisfactory for small databases which are a few GB in size. This is because the time taken to *Backup* is short and the database can be shut off during this period. In *Nonarchivelog* mode, the last consistent whole *Backup* is restored and the database is opened with *Resetlogs* option. No recovery is done. All changes, if any, made after the last *Backup* are lost.

For *Cold Backup*, the database should be *shutdown* under *Shutdown Normal* command. Otherwise, the database should be restarted, *shutdown* with *Normal Shutdown* command and then *backed up*. In the *Cold Backup*, the *Datafiles*, *Control* file, *Online Redolog* files and *Initn.Ora* files have to be *backed up*. The location of all these files can be found from the following *Views*:

Dba_Data_Files/V$datafile/V$logfile/V$controlfile. These *Views* can be queried when the database is *Mounted* but not *Opened*.

7.3   Warm Backup

However, large data warehouses (with hundreds of GB size), such as Credit Card Databases, are very common now-a-days and they are in constant use. They take very long time to *Cold Backup* fully and one can not afford to *shutdown* the database even for a fraction of this *Backup* time. In such situations, another *backup* called *Warm Backup*, also known as *Hot Backup*, is resorted to. In *Warm Backup*, the database is kept open and operational for *Users* and the *OS Backup* commands are given. Since transactions are also going on throughout the interval during which *Warm Backup* is going on, the nature of all transactions, and the precise time of commencement and termination of these transactions are recorded in *Logfiles*. Once the *Backup* is complete, this information on the transactions that took place during the *Backup* and got recorded in the *Logfiles* is applied to the *backed up* database. This way, the database is made uptodate and consistent. This means that for *Warm Backup*, the database must be in *Archivelog* mode. The *Redologfiles* are being written to in a cyclic fashion. When all of them are written, the first one will be overwritten. At this juncture, the information on the *Redologfiles* has to be sent over to the disk or tape for *archiving*. Otherwise since overwriting without *archiving* is not permitted (because it results in loss of valuable information), the database comes to a standstill.

Let us understand how *Warm Backup* works. Assume there are 5 *Datafiles*, F1 to F5, each of which takes 2 hrs to *Backup* and the *Backup* interval is denoted by (B). A changed file due to *User* interaction is denoted by (C). Between t = 0 to t = 10 hrs, the situation is shown in Illustration 7.1. F1 got *backed up* **completely** at t = 2 hrs, F2 at t = 4 hrs and so on. F1 is changed between 6-8 hrs and F4 between 2-4 hrs due to *Updates* etc.

At the end of 10 hrs, the *backed up* files will look like that depicted in Illustration 7.2

Time in hours	Data file1	Data file2	Data file3	Data file4	Data file5
0-2	F1(B)	F2	F3	F4	F5
2-4	F1	F2(B)	F3	F4(C)	F5
4-6	F1	F2	F3(B)	F4(C)	F5
6-8	F1(C)	F2	F3	F4(B)(C)	F5
8-10	F1(C)	F2	F3	F4(C)	F5(B)
At 10	F1(C)	F2	F3	F4(C)	F5

Illustration 7.1 - Backup Situation at Different Times

10 hrs	F1	F2	F3	F4(C)	F5

Illustration 7.2 - Backup Situation After 10 hrs

At t = 10 hrs, out of the five *Datafiles*, two (F1 and F4) changed in the original. But the *backed up* file missed the F1 change because the file *Backup* was completed at t = 2 hrs with no change at the time of its *Backup* (< 2 hrs) and the change took place between t = 6 hrs and t = 8 hrs, much later than its *Backup*. So the *backed up* file does not reflect the changed F1. On the other hand, F4 was changed during 2-4 hrs and its *Backup* took place during 6-8 hrs, much later than changed situation. So the *backed up* file reflects the changed F4.

At the end of 10 hrs *Backup*, the *Logfile* recorded two changes, F1 to F1(C) and F4 to F4(C). Oracle looks at F1 in the *Backup* file and notices that it was not changed. So it applies that change and corrects F1 to F1(C). There is one more change. It looks at F4 and notices that it was already incorporated in F4(C). So no correction is required.

The *backed up* version, after applying *Logfile* information, will appear as shown in Illustration 7.3, which is consistent.

F1(C)	F2	F3	F4(C)	F5

Illustration 7.3 - Backup Situation After Redologfile Application

In order to find out if a file in the database is in *Backup* mode or not, the following command is issued:

```
SQL> Select * from V$backup;
```

The result will look like that in Illustration 7.4.

105

File_Id	Status	ChangeNumber	Time
1	Not active	0	06/07/99 00.00.00
2	Not active	0	06/07/99 00.00.00

Illustration 7.4 - Backup Status of Files

That means that the above two files are not being *backed up* at the time mentioned in the last column. The details about the File #1 or 2 can be obtained by querying as follows:

```
SQL>   Select * from Dba_Data_Files
       where File_Id = 1 (or 2);
```

See Section 4.5 and Illustration 4.6.

7.4   Export/Import Utility

It was mentioned earlier that in *Cold/Warm Backup,* even if one *Table* is lost, the entire *Datafile,* i.e., *Tablespace* has to be *backed up* again. To avoid this, Oracle provided *Export (Exp80.exe)/Import (Imp80.exe)* utility. In this utility, *Backup* is performed *Table*-wise in each *Datafile.* The only drawback is that during *Export,* the database should not be transacted. *Export* captures the contents of *Datafiles* but it does not capture their structure. It also does not capture the supporting files such as *Control* file, *Initn.Ora* files and *Redologfiles.* **Hence Export has to be done with database in *Shutdown* state.** The *Redologs* and *Archivelog* should be *Offline.* Since a table size is smaller than that of a *Tablespace*, this *Shutdown* is a small price to pay to *Backup* the *Table.*

The greatest advantage of *Export* is its ability to *backup* data on an object by object basis. It provides a picture (snapshot) of the database as it existed at the time the *Export* started.

Exp/Imp is available in different modes. They are:

106

- **One of the three Incremental/Cumulative/Full modes**:

  Exp Username/Password   Inctype = Incremental   File = Export_Full

  Cumulative

  Complete

- **Table mode:**

  Exp Username/Password *Tables = Table1, Table2*

  File = Export_File_Name

- **User mode:**

  Exp Username/Password   Owner = Schema_Name Rows = n File = Export_File_Name

- **User's objects but not *Grant*s to be exported:**

  Exp Username/Password   Owner = Schema_Name *Grants* = n File = Export_File_Name

In the more recent versions of Oracle, *Export* with *User* concurrent transaction of the database without *shutdown* is possible by using a new option *Consistent* = Yes. In this mode an *RBS* is set apart exclusively to log the changes made to the database during an *Export*. But this slows down the performance of *Export*. There are several options for parameters for *Export*.

The original *Table* should first be exported to a dump file *XYZ.dmp*. The original *Table* is then dropped. To do this, all the referential integrity constraints should be disabled first, the *Table* dropped, the *.dmp Table imported* into the original location and then the integrity constraints enabled again.

While discussing *Exp/Imp*, the following points may be relevant.

- In order to get rid of *Fragmentation*, one resorts to *Export/Import* tools. In this, the *Tablespace* can be exported using *Compress* = Y option along with all *Tables*, *Grants*, *Privileges* etc. to another temporary location. Then all objects in the original *Tablespace* can be *deleted*. The original *Tablespace* location should be empty. Then the entire exported *Tables*, *Grants*, *Privileges* etc can be *imported* back into the empty space. This will get rid of all *Fragmentation* in the *Tablespace.*

- Suppose one is in an *Instance* of a particular *OS* and needs data from some other *Instance* of a different *OS*, *Export* can be used.

- Suppose one has a database on say Oracle 5 or 6 version and wishes to transfer the data to Oracle 6 or 7, then this utility can be used. It may be noted that this type of transferring data from one Oracle version to another must go through one step at a time. Oracle 5 cannot *Export* to Oracle 7 directly. First it has to go to Oracle 6 and then only to Oracle 7.

- The *Export* process goes interactively. Details of *Table/Index* to be *exported* are given in Illustration 7.5.

Owner	Tablespace	Object
URKRao	UR_TAB	Tables
URKRao	UR_IND	Indexes

Illustration 7.5 - Export of Table and Index

In the two *Tablespaces* above, there is only one owner, "URKRao".

Suppose the command to *Export UR_TAB* into *UR.dmp* (dump file) is given, it will ask

Index?   Choose Y

Compress?   Choose Y

Then both *UR_TAB* and *UR_IND* will be copied to the dump file. The original files can be dropped and then *imported* in *Full* mode.

- *Exp* can move a database from one computer to another/from one *OS* to another through *FTP,* or sent to tape/disk since it is a binary file.

- A lost *Datafile* can be recovered by *OS Backup.* A dropped file can be recovered by *Exp/Imp.*

- Since *Clusters* are not included in the *Exp,* it can be used to remove *Clusters* from *Table.*

- *Exp_Full_Database* can *export* full database using the Full = Y option. In this, all database objects except those owned by *Sys* are *exported. Consistent* = Y option in *Export* retains one *RBS* while the data is being *exported* (Section 7.5).

- As mentioned earlier, in *Export* mode, along with the data, *Create Table* scripts are also copied to the dump file. Hence the original *Table* can be safely dropped. It may be added here that on *Export,* the dump file also has information about where in the database (full path) the original file came from. So in *Import,* the *Tables* are *created* in the same place where they were dropped from. In addition, Oracle 7 provides a new parameter *Destroy* (= Y or N) for *Export/Import* among multiple databases. If the database to *exported* to a *.dmp* file, with *Destroy* parameter = Y, the *.dmp* file can be *imported* into a totally new database with a new path.

7.5   RBS for Import

It was mentioned earlier that a *RBS* can be used for *Import* of database. But the main problem is *RBS* has a very small size compared to that of a database. Even if one *imports Table*-wise, the *RBS* should accommodate the entire *Table* contents and this is going to be a large burden on the *RBS.* There is a way to get around this problem. In the *Import* command there is a choice for the size of buffer as well as a choice for the parameter *Commit*

(Yes or No). Depending upon the size of the *RBS* provided, the buffer size can be chosen. Let us say that we chose 64,000 bytes for buffer size and *Commit* = Y. The data is transferred in chunks of 64,000 bytes and then *committed*. This way the problem is solved. If buffer size is inadequate, an IMP.00020 error will be issued. Another advantage of the *Commit* = Y option is that, even if the *Import* fails in the middle of the transfer of a *Table*, still it is possible to *commit* all the data transferred till that failure, ignoring the rest of the *Table*.

7.6   Pitfalls in Export/Import

When *Exp80.exe* is run, it exports *Users* in the order in which they were *created* in the database. If *Users* "Sam", "Anna", "Ram", "Brian" were *created* in that order, the database objects of these *Users* are exported in that order, i.e., first those of "Sam", then those of "Anna" and so on. Let us assume that *Table T1* of "Sam" was *created* much later than *T11* of "Anna", even then all *Tables* of "Sam" including *T1* will be *exported* before all the *Tables* of "Anna" including *T11* are *exported*. Within one *User*, all the *Tables* are *exported* in the alphabetical order of their names. For example in the *User* "Sam's" space, there are two objects, *Table Tell_Hd* and its *View AcctV_Tell_Hd*. Among these, following alphabetical order, the *View* will be *exported* first and then the *Table*. So far there is no complication. This process is identical in *Import*. However, here trouble arises. During *Import* (*Imp80.exe* file run), following alphabetical order, transfer of *AcctV_Tell_Hd* will be attempted before the transfer of *Tell_Hd*. At this juncture, *creation* of the *Table Tell_Hd* would not have taken place. *Create AcctV_Tell_Hd* (*View* of *Tell_Hd*) command depends on the pre-existence of *Tell_Hd*. The error message, ORA.00942, will be issued. Oracle has provided a remedial path for this. During the first *Import*, the *AcctV_Tell_Hd View* will not be *created*. If the *Imp80.exe* file is run a second time, with options *Rows* = N and *Ignore* = N, then the files that got *backed up* in the first run will not be affected and only those like the *View, AcctV_Tell_Hd*, which were not *backed u*p in the first *Imp* round will now get *backed up*.

7.7 Commands For Export/Import

Some of the useful SQL commands pertaining to *Export/Import* are given below.

- **Import from One Account into Another Account**

  Suppose you want to transfer *Datafiles* from the account of *User* "URKRao" to the account of *User* "Ganpat". The following two commands are issued.

  ```
  SQL> Exp System/Manager
       File = URKRao.dmp
       Owner = URKRao Grants = N
       Indexes = Y
       Compress = Y Rows = Y

  SQL> Imp System/Manager
       File = URKRao.dmp
       FROMUSER = URKRao TOUSER = Ganpat
       Rows = Y Indexes = Y
  ```

- **Import using separate *Tables/Indexes***

  Suppose you want to copy "URKRao's" objects into "Samson's" account and the *Indexes* are to be separated from the *Tables*. In that case, the following commands may be used.

  ```
  SQL> EXP System/Manager
       File = URKRao.dmp
       Owner = URKRao IMPSystem/Manager
       File = URKRao.dmp
       IndexFile = UINDEX.SQL
  ```

  (At this juncture, *UINDEX.SQL* is edited to change the *Tablespace* name of the *Indexes* so that its *Index* file does not go to the same destination as the *Table*.)

```
SQL> IMP System/manager File URKRao.dmp
     FROMUSER URKRao TOUSER  Samson
     Index = N Commit = Y Buff = 64000
```

```
SQL*PLUS> @UINDEX.SQL;
```

This will *create* the *Index* file separately.

7.8   Comparison of Different Backup Methods

The use and limitations of *Backup* methods are given in the Illustration 7.6.

Method	Nature	Capability	Application
Exp/Imp	Exp/Imp	Can recover the database to its status when the backup commenced	If a Table or two need backup, this is good. Ideal for object level backup
Cold Backup	Physical	Can recover the database to the point where it was shutdown	Ideal at or higher than Tablespace level. Suitable for small databases only.
Warm Backup	Physical	Can recover a database at any point of time to its consistent level	Ideal for large databases with high transaction density.

Illustration 7.6 - Comparison of Backup Methods

7.9   Warm Backup Commands

Warm Backup is possible only when the database is running in the *Archivelog* mode, i.e., the database is open and *Archivelogs* are started. For that, the *Log_Archive_Start* parameter in the *Initn.Ora* file must first be assigned a value of "TRUE". The database must be *shutdown* and the *Instance* should be restarted. Then the *Archivelogs* will be *Online*. The following are the sequence of commands.

```
SQL> SQLDBA lmode = Y

SQL> Startup Mount Database_Name;

SQL> Alter database Archivelog;

SQL> Archivelog start;

SQL> Alter database open;
```

7.9.1   Warm Backup Begin/End

```
SVRMGR> Alter Tablespace Ts_Name
        begin backup;
 (perform backup of Ts_Name by OS now)

SVRMGR> Alter Tablespace Ts_Name end backup;
```

After this, the archived *Redologfiles* are to be *backed up*.

It may be noted that the *Control* file can not be *backed up* by any utility.

```
SVRMGR> Alter database backup
        Controlfile to 'file_name';
```

Control **file should always be *backed up* after every structural change to the database.** Once the database is in *Archivelog* mode, it may be *backed up* while being transacted by *User*s. One should ensure that adequate size for *Archivelogs* is provided. At the end of *Warm Backup*, the database is to be returned to *Non-archivelog* mode (Original Status). The commands are:

```
SQL> SQLDBA lmode = y

SQL> Connect Internal;

SQL> Startup Mount Database_Name;

SQL> Alter database Noarchivelog;

SQL> Alter database open;
```

There are readymade scripts available for *Backups* including those of *System/ RBS/Data/Indexes and Temp Tablespaces* in addition to those of *Redologfiles, Control* file. Again, at any time, during *Warm Backup*, it should be ensured that the *Archivelog* destination has adequate storage space

It is a matter of common sense that *Warm Backup* be scheduled to times when there is minimum traffic on the database for *User* transactions. Otherwise, the *OS* will be flooded with commands both from the *Backup* as well as from the *Users* resulting in *contention.*

7.10 Recovery

After a full *Warm Backup*, the database should be checked and validated for the recovery, i.e., *Consistency.* Even after you have decided the mode of *Backup* and *Recovery,* and are ready with the scripts, you should never test the B*ackup* process with real data in the first attempt. Test data should be generated and the *Backup* and *Recovery* processes should be applied on that data. A duplicate copy of that data should be available to avoid total loss of data in case of a failure. The failure may not necessarily be due to faulty *Backup*, it might arise out of many other reasons such as disk problems.

Even after successful testing on test data, it is still desirable to have a duplicate copy of the real data, before applying the *Backup*.

7.11 Standby Database

A standby database is a duplicate copy of the database to save the situation, in case disaster strikes the database. **The standby database is in constant state of** *recovery*.

7.12 Instance Failure

Before creating database, *Backup* and *Recovery* plan should be planned for the business needs of the database. Different types of failures are possible. They are enumerated below.

- **Media failure**: This occurs when files needed can no longer be accessed due to disk drive failure.

- **Statement failure**: *Users* may issue queries with syntax errors. Oracle handles such situations with error message. No *recovery* is needed.

- **Process failure**: Such failures arise out of network failure/client-side power failure/*User*-killed client process. The Oracle *PMON* process automatically recovers such failed processes.

- **Instance failure**: They are caused by power outages/*OS* crash/Any Oracle process death/*Instance* death. The Oracle process *SMON* recovers the *Instance* in such conditions

- **Disk failure**: Such failures are a result of disk drive failure and the standard *Backup* methods provide the remedy.

- **User drop of** *Table*: If a *User* inadvertently drops a *Table*, suitable *Backup* methods exist to handle such situations.

There may be an *Instance* crash due to any number of reasons. While restarting the *Instance*, it recovers after accessing *Control* file, *Online Redologfiles* and of course *Datafiles*. As mentioned earlier, all vital files should be available in duplicate. Many *DBAs* have four copies of *Control* file, since it is extremely important if the *Instance* fails. The *Online Redologs* should also be mirrored. For obvious reasons each of these mirrored files should be on a different disk.

7.13   Role of DBA

It is very difficult to exactly specify the *Role* of a *DBA*. However, generally speaking, the following jobs fall in the realm of an *Oracle DBA*.

* Installation and Upgradation

* Designing, *Creating* and *Altering* Database as per Application specification.

* Creating Primary storage (*Tablespace* etc)

* Creating Primary database objects such as Schema objects.

* Main Oracle Licence Compliance.

* Enrolling *Users* and providing rights

* Archiving Files (*Backup*)

* Periodic *Backup*

* *Recovery*

* Performance Tuning

* Laison with Oracle Corporation for technical feed back on bugs, upgrades etc.

Chapter 8   Audit

We have just seen that Oracle provides security at several levels down to the column level of a *Table*. By and large, to be practicable, many of the common *Privileges* have to be *granted* to several *Users*. For example, *DBA Privileges* like *Backup* are to be given to non-*DBA*s so that the job does gets done on time. Some *Users* may cross the limits of their *Privileges* and may tread a path which is not in the best interests of the organization which owns the database. An unscrupulous *User* may use his *Privilege* to collect and pass on vital information to the competitors. In order to have a surveillance of the database activities of such *Users*, *Audit,* provided by Oracle, may be used. Besides, as a routine monitoring of the different activities of the database, *Audit* can be used to collect information about the traffic in different activities on the database. It can *audit* all activities that take place within the database.

Audit is like a utility. It is not done routinely when the database is opened since it slows down its performance. In order to enable *Audit*, in Oracle 7 the *Audit_Trail* parameter of the *Initn.Ora* file has to be assigned a value "OB" (equal to "TRUE"). The resulting *Audit* information is written to a *Table* known as *Sys.Aud$*. In some *OS*s, the *Audit* information can be collected in a *OS* file. Again like *Privileges, Audit action* can be fine-tuned. The *Audit* functionality can be modified at will. For example, in *auditing Login* attempts, both successful and unsuccessful ones can be recorded separately. If an unauthorised person tries to login, it will show up in the *Audit*.

8.1   Session Audit

The first command to commence *Audit* is:

```
> Audit Session;
```

In order to differentiate between the successful and unsuccessful ones, two separate calls are possible:

```
> Audit Session Whenever Successful;
> Audit Session Whenever Not Successful;
```

The *Table Sys_Aud$* has columns as follows:

Session_Id/Entry_Id/Statements/TimeStampNo/User_Id/
TerminalActionNo/Returncode/Obj$Creator/Object$name/
Auth$Priv/Auth$Granter/New$Owner/New$Name/Ses$Actions/
Ses$TID/Logoff$Lread/Logoff$Lwrite/Logoff$Dead/Logoff$Time/
Logoff$Text/Logoff$Spare1/Logoff$Spare2/Obj$Label/Ses$Label/
Priv$Used

Based on the information in *Sys.Aud$*, a *View Dba_Audit_Session* is populated. This *View* has the following 14 columns:

OS_Username/User_Name/User_Host/Terminal/Timestamp/
Action_Name/Logoff_Time/Logoff_Lread/Logoff_Pread/
Logoff_Lwrite/Logoff_Dlock/Session_Id/Return_Code/
Session_Label

Suppose one would like to know the number of times an account was logged into both successfully and unsuccessfully along with session times (if logged in). Then the following query answers this:

```
SQL> Select OS_Username, User_Name,Terminal,
     decode(returncode,'0',
     'Connected','1005',
     'FailedNull','1017', 'Failed',
     returncode), To_char(timestamp,
     'DD-MON-YY HH24:MI:SS'),
     To_char(Logoff_Time,
     'DD-MON-YY HH24:MI:SS')
     from Dba_Audit_Session;
```

Returncode 0 indicates successful login. Timestamp in the above query denotes Login time. 1015 is ORA error indicating absence of password and 1017 is another ORA error indicating invalid password..

To close the *Session Audit*, the command is:

```
SQL> Noaudit Session;
```

8.2   Object Action Audit

Any action such as *Create, Alter* that affects a database object (*Table, Index, RBS* etc) can be *audited*. All *Sys*tem-level commands can be *audited* individually.

For every *action*, the call for *Audit* is:

```
SQL> Audit action;
```

The call to terminate the *Audit action* is:

```
SQL> Noaudit action;
```

The command *Audit Role* takes care of all actions of *Role* such as *Create Role, Drop Role, Set Role.*

Individual actions that can be *audited* are identified in the *View Audit_Actions* by a numerical number.

The following query gives the action code number identifying all the *actions* for *Audit.*

```
SQL> Select action, name
        from Audit_Actions;
```

There are 121 rows in the output of which three are given in Illustration 8.1.

Action	Name
1	Create
2	Insert
3	Delete

Illustration 8.1 - Typical Output of the Table Audit_Actions

Suppose you would like to track down the action on a particular database object (For example I would like to know who did *Deletes* on my database object, *Tell_Hd*, a *Table)*, then the *Dba_Audit_Object View* can be queried via the following command.

```
SQL> Select Os_Name, Username, Terminal,
     Owner, Obj_Name,Action_Name,
     decode(returncode,'0',
     'Success', returncode),
     To_char(Timestamp,
     'DD_MM-YY H24:MI:SS')
     from Dba_Audit_Object;
```

```
(For my Table where Owner = 'URKRao'
 and  Obj_Name  =  'Tell_Hd',  Action_Name  =
'DELETE';).
```

If there is a suspicion that any particular *User* ("Gopal") has been tampering with *Tables* by changing values in the columns, specifically "Gopal's" *actions* on all *Tables* can be *audited* by the following command.

```
SQL> Audit Update by Gopal;
```

This will pinpoint all *Update* actions of "Gopal" on all *Tables*. Any action (*Update* etc) on any *User*'s ("URKRao's") database objects can be *audited* as follows:

```
SQL> Audit Update on URKRao.Tell_Hd;
```

This will *audit* all *Update* activities on *URKRao.Tell_Hd Table*.

If *Audit* can record all *actions* on the database objects, how about the *actions* on the *Sys.Aud$*?

One can tamper with the *Audit* records by *altering* the records of *Sys.Aud$* itself. If anybody tries to tamper with this *Audit View*, can we track him down? That is, can the Police be policed? The answer is yes. The following command does it.

```
SQL> Audit all on Sys.Aud$ by Access;
```

So all attempts to tamper with this *View* will be recorded. *DBAs* can delete any records of the *View*, but that *action* will also be recorded. So one can see the tremendous foresight of Oracle Security planners.

Chapter 9   Application Tuning

9.1   Introduction

Very few programmers realise that the code they write for an application may not be the most efficient one in terms of speed and efficiency, inspite of the best resources offered by the *Instance* they run their program on. Oftentimes, very minor changes in the code might improve its ability to tap all the advantages offered by the resources. The situation may be compared with an automobile vis-a-vis road. Assume that you are given an expensive fast automobile (an *Instance* with good resources). You have all the resources to go fast safely even while negotiating curves and arrive at the destination within a very short time. However, if the roads are badly paved and have lots of potholes (application with poorly written code), you can never utilise the resources of the automobile to reach the speed attainable and will not be able to reach the destination within the time that it would have taken, had all the resources been used.   Therefore it would be better if the Application programmer consults with the *DBA* to ensure that the program will be able to maximise the usage of resources in the *Instance.*

When programmers find that all bugs in their code are removed, and the code is running without any errors, they feel satisfied with the code and its outcome. However, it should be realised that in Oracle there are innumerable ways in which code can be written for a given application and the desired output can be obtained without any errors.   The most important aspect of the whole business is obtaining the desired goal at the best possible pace and with optimum usage of the resources. Different types of code consume different extents of resources. The most economical usage of the resources is desired.

In this discussion we present mistakes (not arising out of syntax) in the code of the first version our Integrated Bank Branch Management Application (IBBM), its effect on the performance of the *Instance* and the way they were rectified.

9.2   Interest Calculation

In our IBBM application, there was one module in which the bank interest payable to different types of accounts such as *Savings, Over-Drafts, Cash-Credit, Fixed-Deposit-Receipts, Jewellery-Loan* etc was computed. For example, for the *Savings* accounts, the computation for each account was done by an appropriate arithmetic equation and the result was *inserted* into a *Table*. The computation for all the accounts in *Savings* was done within a loop and then the *Commit* command was issued for the whole set of *Inserts* in the *Table* for *Savings*. While this operation was being performed, all other *Users* of the *Instance* started reporting that their applications were slowing. The following changes in our IBBM application alleviated the problem.

9.2.1   Sort

The *Tell_Hd* and *Tell_Det Tables* carried all the data required for the interest calculations for all types of accounts. These two *Tables* in our database of accounts had a composite *Primary Key* (Acctcode, Acctno). However, the data was not exactly in the order of these two keys. This was so because, although to start with, the data was *inserted* in the order in which the *Primary Key* was reflected, some of the entries were later found to be wrong. They were then deleted and reinserted with correct values thereby disturbing the order. Thus if one issued the command:

```
SQL> Select  Acctcode, Acctno
     from Tell_Det where Acctcode = 1
     and Acctno  = <10;
```

The order of records retrieved was as shown in Illustration 9.1.

Acctcode	Acctno
1	1
1	2
1	4
1	5
1	8
1	3
1	6
1	9
1	10
1	7

Illustration 9.1 - Acctcode, Acctno Output from the Database

The data in the database was in the order of *Acctcode* but not in the order of Acctno. If the data was to be retrieved for *Acctcode* = 1 and Acctno = 7, the advantage of using the composite *Primary Key* was lost since the search had to go through the entire database. Hence there was inefficiency built into the application program. This could have been avoided if the data was sorted. By using *Exp/Imp* utility, the data was *exported, sorted* as per the *Primary Key* and then *imported* back. This improved the situation.

9.2.2 Interchange of columns of Primary Key in Select Statement

In addition, we did not take proper care in formatting our *Select* statements. In some places "where Acctno = x and Acctcode = y " was used whereas elsewhere the sequence was changed and "where Acctcode = y and Acctno = x" was used. This is not correct and one has to use the *where* clause with Acctcode and Acctno in the same sequence in which the *Primary Key* was defined and should not be interchanged.

9.2.3   Function

The next improvement was made by introducing suitable functions instead of equations for calculating the interest for each type of account. The function for each type was stored in compiled form and reused for each Acctno in that Acctcode. This reduced the time of computation and improved the situation further.

9.2.4   Commit

As mentioned earlier, the computation of interest for a given Acctcode was done Acctno-wise, the result inserted into a *Table* and the process was repeated in a loop until all Acctnos were exhausted and then *committed*. Since there were many accounts, this resulted in eating up of all the *RBS* resources in the shared *Instance* and locking it up for a considerable amount of time. This was the principal culprit responsible for slowing down all other *Users'* jobs within the *Instance*. As discussed earlier, our application program was modified to *commit* about 100 Acctnos at a time thereby reducing the size of the *RBS*. This further improved the situation.

These are a few examples where minor modifications to the Application Program resulted in exploiting fully the resources offered by the *Instance* rather than burdening it.

Thus, by and large it may be concluded that the overall performance of an Oracle *Instance* depends critically on all team players, viz., *DBAs, Users and Application programmers* and it is essential that each appreciates the complementary *role* played by the other and tries to understand the requirements of the others.

Index